PROJECT
MANAGEMENT
for MANAGERS

INTERIOR HEALTH AUTHORITY
Financial Services
104-1815 Kirschner Road
Kelowna, BC V1Y 4N7

PROJECT MANAGEMENT
for MANAGERS

Mihály Görög
Nigel J. Smith

Project Management Institute

Library of Congress Cataloging-in-Publication Data

Görög, Mihály, 1951–
   Project management for managers / Mihály Görög, Nigel J. Smith.
        p.   cm.
   Includes bibliographical references (p.   ) and index.
   ISBN: 1-880410-54-0 (alk. paper)
   1. Industrial project management. 2. Industrial development
projects--Study and teaching. I. Smith, Nigel J. II. Title.
   HD69.P75G67 1998
   658.4′04 - - dc21   98–40818
                                                                 CIP

Published by: Project Management Institute Headquarters
                  Four Campus Boulevard, Newtown Square, Pennsylvania 19073-3299 USA
                  Phone: 610-356-4600 or Visit our website: www.pmi.org

ISBN: 1-880410-54-0

PMI Book Team
Editor-in-Chief, James S. Pennypacker
Editor, Toni D. Knott
Assistant Editor, Lisa M. Fisher
Graphic Designer (text), Michelle T. Owen
Graphic Designer (cover), Allison S. Boone
Acquisitions Editor, Bobby R. Hensley
Production Coordinator, Mark S. Parker

PMI books are available at special quantity discounts to use as premiums and sales
promotions, or for use in corporate training programs. For more information, please
write to the Business Manager, PMI Publishing Division, Forty Colonial Square, Sylva,
NC 28779 USA. Or contact your local bookstore.

The paper used in this book complies with the Permanent Paper Standard issued by the
National Information Standards Organization (Z39.48—1984).

PMBOK™ is a trademark and PMP® is a registered certification mark of the
Project Management Institute.

10 9 8 7 6 5 4 3 2 1

CONTENTS

FIGURES

Tables

PREFACE

PROJECTS AND PROJECT MANAGEMENT as the way of realizing an *ad hoc* task—such as constructing a facility, developing a new product, or introducing some new services—have existed ever since people began to collaborate many centuries ago. Even though the practitioners then were not aware of acting as project managers, they were coping with all of the problems of projects and all of the functions of project management. Managing projects in a predetermined manner evolved in the late 1940s, mainly due to the experience gained in trying to control the vastly expensive weapon system development and space exploration programs. During these decades, many newly introduced technical tools (network planning techniques and cost control methods) improved the practice of project management, while the academic paradigm pertaining to project management did not change. At this time, project management was considered to be a collection of *add-on* techniques rather than a distinct management discipline.

Due to the accelerating changes in both the macroeconomic and environmental characteristics over the last decade, it has been gradually realized that projects are building elements in the strategy implementation of organizations. This implies that there is a need for project-oriented strategic management; i.e., organizational strategies should define the associated projects, as well. At the same time, it implies the need for strategy-oriented project management, too; for example, projects should be initiated and implemented in accordance with the organizational strategic objectives. These changes were influential in the emergence of a new paradigm for managing projects, which can be referred to as strategic-oriented project management. This new paradigm in project management implies the following.

- The project cycle encompasses, among others, the transformation of strategic objectives into projects, on the one hand, and the post-evaluation of the project implementation from the point of view of strategies, on the other hand.
- Along with improvement of the technical tools, development of the methodological background of managing projects is in the forefront.
- Instead of implementing single isolated projects, interrelated projects are to be implemented within an organization.

This book focuses on strategic-oriented project management and identifying the role of project management in the organization. Many project management books concentrate on describing different techniques and tools while virtually ignoring the problem of using the most appropriate in the case of a given project or situation.

This book is not concerned with techniques and tools in detail; rather, it concentrates on methodology of decision-making involving the use of project management techniques and tools.

The majority of project management textbooks concentrate on a certain industry (e.g., construction) or on certain type of projects (e.g., R&D). This book abandons the narrow outlook and introduces approaches and methods that are applicable to all projects. Instead of concentrating on sector-specific case studies, the book emphasizes the rationale and philosophy of project management.

This book is written for both students and practitioners. It is partially dedicated to graduate and postgraduate students in the field of management and engineering management, M.B.A.'s, and participants in executive programs. The book is also dedicated to practitioners who are responsible for managing change within an organization.

Although project management is more and more a distinct discipline, at the same time, owing to its inevitable strategy orientation, it is an integrated part of the management sciences. That is why the authors have chosen the title, *Project Management for Managers*.

Mihály Görög	Nigel J. Smith
Chapters 1–3	Chapter 4
Chapters 5–6	Chapters 7–9
Chapters 10–12	Chapters 13–14

ACKNOWLEDGEMENTS

W E, THE AUTHORS of this book, would like to thank all past and present colleagues and our students. Both staff and students provided valuable criticism and comments throughout workshop discussions and project management lecture courses.

We are particularly grateful to our families for providing a stable background for our efforts in the course of developing this book.

Finally, we would especially like to thank Ms. Adrienne Pósvai and Mr. László Mészöly in Budapest, and Ms. Sally Mortimer and Dr. Kareem Yusuf in Leeds for processing and improving the draft versions of the different chapters, and for transforming our sketches into figures and tables.

Chapter One

The Role of Project
Management in Organizations

THESE DAYS IT seems commonplace to announce that life has
accelerated. It is commonplace but nonetheless true that in the
second half of the Twentieth Century the need for almost nonstop
change has become a mode of existence both in social and economic organizations. This need in the life of different organizations
implies that they will always be required to carry out something
new, some one-off activity that is different from the daily assignments that they have to complete during a certain period. Thus, in
order to achieve their strategic objectives and adapt themselves to
the almost continuously changing environmental conditions, organizations have to implement different projects. This contributes to
the fact that project management has assumed a new and significant
role in managing companies. David I. Cleland emphasizes what has
been said so far: "Project management constitutes one of the main
forms for converting an organization from one state to another. It
might be called *transitional management*" (1994, 34).

In this chapter, based on the ideas expressed above, the authors
will introduce the place and role of project management within
organizations. Light will be shed on management dimensions
existing in organizations and the interweaving between organizational strategy and projects. Further, attempts will be made, based
on certain principles, to categorize different kinds of projects.

Management Dimensions in Organizations

An organization—whether it is profit oriented or a government
organization in the service of the public sector—is in every case des-
tined to carry out a task that can be more or less defined. Such a task

1

has to be implemented day by day and could be the production and selling of products, fulfillment of certain services, or other functions.

The daily activities of an operating organization, and the terms and conditions under which the implementation of these activities is carried out, are shaped and determined both in the long and short term by the internal characteristics of the organization and the external environment. If the internal and external characteristics go through changes, they prompt change in the daily activities of the organization, such as the modification of a previously manufactured product or perhaps the introduction of new, not previously manufactured products or services. In the majority of cases, however, not only the daily activities go through modifications, but the terms and conditions of the implementation of these activities within the organization also undergo changes. For example, new technologies are applied, new production capacities come to the forefront, new markets are acquired, and new organizational structures and new owners or new forms of ownership are brought forth. The term *technologies* is used in its broadest sense, and implies many procedures that describe a given process. Amid these changes, however, the organization continuously implements the daily activities and tasks of the given period. This duality in the operation of organizations—the execution of daily activities in relatively stable internal conditions in the short term, and the changing and/or the transformation of the circumstances of this execution in the long term—illustrates that managing an organization is a multifunctional activity.

One of the functions of managing a company is to ensure that the daily activities are implemented continuously and efficiently. For example, purchasing and stockpiling, manufacturing, assembling, quality control, warehousing, and selling—then again, financial, accounting, and other administrative activities associated with these activities—constitute daily assignments at a company utilizing mass production. In this dimension, management can be referred to as *operating management.*

Besides the constant realization of the daily activities, the company's management must face change. Upon assuming this role, the management has to be able, based on the likely changes of the external forces and on the internal characteristics, to define the company's future development direction. In other words, the management has to outline a vision to be fulfilled, which will contribute to or ensure the survival of the company. It goes without saying that as the external and internal characteristics of the organization are modified, similarly the management can shape, more or less continuously, the future development direction of the organization. Consequently, consecutive but not necessarily contradictory goals can be outlined in the organization's mission and vision. In this dimension, management can be referred to as *strategic management*.

If the management of the organization outlines a realistic vision, which is used as a basis for defining realistic strategic goals, the ability of the company to operate well in the future largely depends on how the strategic objectives are implemented. Once they are implemented, the results are incorporated into the daily activities and exert great influence on the efficient running of the organization. To achieve the organization's vision, several strategic goals and objectives are simultaneously defined, while the implementation of them often takes place either in parallel or in series; sometimes they even overlap with each other. The implementation of strategic goals and objectives may take place not only at different times but also could be different in content, for example, the development of a new product and introducing it into the market. Implementation of these tasks lead the organization's management to approaches, methods, and techniques different from those of operating and strategic management; that is why, in this dimension, management can be referred to as *project management*.

This threefold manifestation of managing an organization can be observed in every organization, although there are a number of cases when it does not shine through the organizational structure. For example, these functions are not separated in small companies. Yet, from the point of view of big organizations, the functions surrounding setting strategies and project and operating management can be observed in the organizational structure.

Thus, project management is a kind of category in between the strategic and operating levels of management and, as such, it is responsible for the implementation of strategic objectives. It also provides the means for transforming strategic objectives into daily activities. In this sense, project management is a means for implementing strategy, while the project itself is a defined strategic program or a part of it, a strategic action, or a well-definable part of the actions.

In order to understand the interrelation between strategy and project management, the basics of strategy and strategy formulation should be briefly reviewed. When setting strategies, the management of an organization tries to find answers to such question as the following.

- Based on the present and likely terms and conditions of the external forces and the internal characteristics of the organization, what kind of a future position seems to be reasonable?
- What kinds of decisions have to be made in order to achieve the expected position?

3

■ What kinds of means (resources, methods, and so on) are required in order to realize the decision?

In accordance with this, it can be seen that organizational strategies bring about a kind of hierarchic structure, which is made up of the following typical elements (see Figure 1.1).

Vision and mission can be considered as a general statement indicating the future activities and position of the organization (*justification* for the existence of the organization). Thus, it focuses on the long-term operations of the organization (e.g., defining the scope of activities in which the organization will operate and how it will operate).

■ *Goals* ensure that the vision can be achieved and the mission can be fulfilled in certain fields of activity in the organization; therefore, they render a kind of focal point for the organization's resource utilization. Goals are generally qualitative in nature; for example, the organization wants to take the leading position in the development of new products in a given industry.

■ *Objectives* are tasks that can often be defined as quantitative in nature. They ensure the implementation of the goals, thus creating milestones against which they can be measured (e.g., the modernization of laboratories and test areas, which until 1998 were the means for gaining competitive advantage).

■ *Strategies* (strategic programs and actions) are programs of a quantitative nature, and their fulfillment results directly in the realization of the objectives (e.g., construction and installation of new testing areas until 1998).

Organizational strategy is first concerned with the future, and, as such, partly or wholly aims to modify both the operation and the internal characteristics of the organization. Consequently, strategy inherently aims to bring about something that did not previously exist in the organization at the time that the strategies were set. The things to be brought about are defined in the strategic programs and actions, which are the building blocks of the organizational strategy. They imply that *single and complex tasks* have to be implemented *within a given time period* (a deadline or a duration time to be met by the organization) and *within given cost constraints*. In this manner, strategic actions fall in line with basic project characteristics.

The above-mentioned similarity explains why current thinking maintains that the most effective means for strategy implementation is project management. It goes without saying, however, that project management is not a panacea. Rather, it implies exercising a management function in a way that centralizes human and material resources, information, and relevant methodological and technical tools to achieve successful implementation of the defined project result. A project manager is responsible for the implementation of the project and, ideally, is the person with authority.

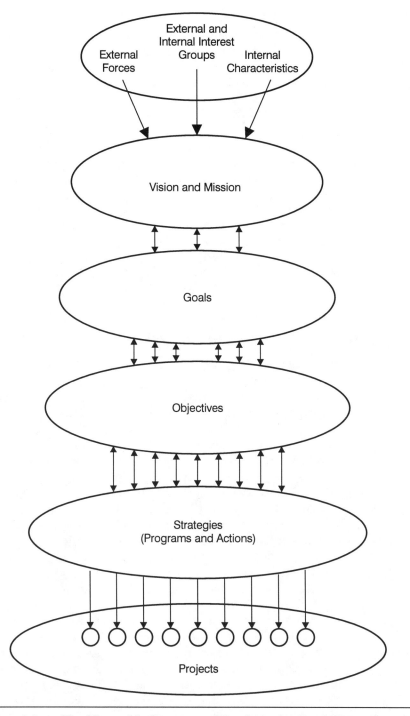

Figure 1.1   The Hierarchic Structure of the Organizational Strategy

In summary, it can be said that there are three basic dimensions or roles in the management of organizations: operating, strategic, and project management. Operating management ensures the smooth flow of activities that currently exist in the organization. Strategic management is responsible for the organization's likely future state, and strategy formulation is also conducted more or less continuously or at regular intervals. The impact of strategic management on operating management is obvious; strategic management tries to change the subject and the conditions of long-term everyday operation. At the same time, operating management provides strategic management with a number of options or predictions for future development.

As long as the activities of both operating and strategic management can be considered continuous in time and, in a given sense of the term, repetitive, project management concentrates on achieving one single particular result. Its time constraints (beginning and end) and cost constraints (resource utilization) are set in advance, and these are the features that have made project management a distinct part of the management sciences.

Organizational Strategy and Projects

Organizational strategy, as a hierarchically built system, sets the long-term development direction of the organization so that it adjusts the operation more or less continuously to the environmental conditions, and to the likely future changes effected by the internal characteristics of the organization. Meanwhile, it has to meet and exert influence on the expectation of the external and internal interest groups. External groups can be considered part of the environment, while internal groups can be perceived as the internal characteristics of the organization. Thus, strategy is nothing more than an answer to the challenges of the environment, i.e., a form of adjustment to environmental changes. The management of an organization, acting in the strategic-management function, has to meet the requirement of the previous demand in order to ensure conditions within the organization necessary for fulfilling the mission and achieving the vision.

Strategic management should meet expectations if strategic analysis, strategy formulation, and formulating the conditions of strategy implementation come to the forefront during strategy setting. The final goal of strategic analysis is to identify the factors of key importance defining the present and future environmental terms and conditions, as well as the present and future position of the organization based on the important environmental factors. Consequently, the analysis has to be concerned with the following:

- external forces, which partly imply the international and domestic macro-environment (political, economic, legal, social, technological, and so on), and further on the industry environment (new entrants, bargaining power of buyers and suppliers, substitutes, positioning of existing competitors); certain elements of the external environment offer possibilities for survival and growth of the company while others act as restrictive forces over competitiveness (M. E. Porter (1979) goes into detail when analyzing the effect that the industry environment exerts on competitive strategy.)
- internal characteristics of the organization (human, technical, financial, management, and so on), which serve as a source of strengths or weaknesses and limit the strategic potential of the organization
- expectations of the external and internal interest groups (shareholders, creditors, consumers, employees, managers, environmental groups, and so on)—owing to the influence that they may exert on the organization, these groups can modify the strategy even amid the strategy implementation and in spite of the unchanging conditions.

Figure 1.2 shows the structure and scope of strategic analyses. This is the scope of activity that more or less comes under the influence of the external and internal interest groups during the course of strategy formulation.

While formulating the strategy, the strategic options and behavior to be followed are elaborated, making it possible for the internal characteristics to match the external characteristics partly or wholly in accordance with interest groups' expectations. The outcome of the strategic analyses serves as the starting point of this activity, and the process itself takes shape through a series of steps.

- Step 1—analysis and evaluation of strategies in order to ensure that they are in accordance with the mission and vision. The analysis should encompass the resources to be acquired or those at the disposal of the organization, which are necessary for strategy implementation.
- Step 2—the decision to be made about strategic options and behavior to be followed. What is characteristic here is that the outcome of the activity can be considerably influenced by the external and internal interest groups. The decision, however, anticipates the strategic objectives (programs and actions) to be implemented.
- Step 3—from the point of view of strategy implementation, the most important milestone of strategy formulation is the development of strategic programs and actions and eventually the formation of projects, since they constitute the means for strategy implementation. The more the result to be achieved can be quantified, the easier it is to implement the strategic objectives. Simultaneously, with the quantitative specification of the desired result, the resource demands—i.e., the cost and time constraints for implementation of the objectives—have to be fixed. Beyond this,

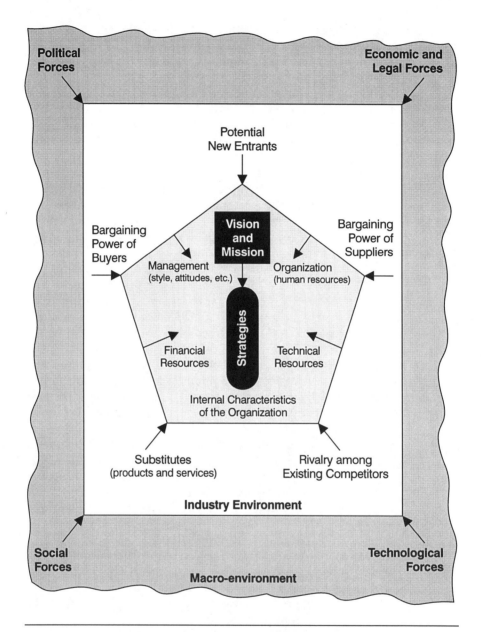

Figure 1.2   The Structure and Scope of Strategic Analyses

however, there are some further conditions—such as detailed structure and time plans of the action, resource allocation, monitoring and controlling, organizational forms, and so on—that have to be decided. The topics mentioned here will be expanded in more project-related detail in later chapters of the book.

It should be noted that, in some of the cases, strategy formulation goes through the sequential steps described above, but, taking it as a whole, we can see that reciprocity (returning to a previous step) is the concomitant of strategy formulation.

The strategy of implementation at the level of strategic programs and actions implies the realization of different complex results, while the external conditions and the internal characteristics of the organization, which are decisive for the strategy as a whole, as well as the expectations of the interest groups, may also change. Consequently, while continuous updating and developing of strategy is essential, the implementation of the settled strategic objectives exhibits a kind of relative stability. These interrelations support the fact that the implementation of strategic actions demands a management approach different from one concerned with strategy formulation and from one building on the general conditions of strategy implementation.

When strategic actions aim at achieving a given result, they suggest the implementation of some complex one-time activity in the organization. To implement such a target—one we have dealt with before—is different from the organization's daily operating activities, and is also different from the approach that considers strategy formulation as an absolutely future-oriented activity encompassing the entire organization as a whole. From the point of view of the organization, such complex, single tasks can be considered projects, and the management activities relating to their implementation are called project management.

Strategy sets the changes for the organization, changes that can be achieved by implementing different kinds of projects. Projects and project management provide the means for the implementation of organizational changes. Projects, simultaneous with project management, provide the tools for the realization of organizational changes; i.e., projects derive from organizational strategies so that they are generated by strategic objectives. This has been the perception over the past few years, although the obvious relationship between strategy and projects existed irrespective of this perception, since change is concomitant to every organization (government, business, social, and so on). What brought this perception to the forefront, however, is the extent to which change in the past decades has speeded up. Cleland views this interweaving as follows: "The existence of projects in organizations is one clear indication that the organization is changing and is attempting to meet changing future environments. This is a key point not to be missed by senior managers and directors" (1994, 118).

The existence of projects in an organization is closely related to organizational strategy. Projects are the building elements of organizational strategy. The more projects that are implemented by an organization in a given period, the more certain it is that the company is undergoing change because it wishes to adapt itself, in accordance with its strategy, to changing environmental forces.

It can be said that projects are brought into being and shaped by the organizational strategy, while project management is a management function responsible for the implementation of projects. These two management functions are in a sense connected by the project itself; the differences, however, can be traced from the diverging scope of authority of the two functions, relating to project implementation.

In order to gain a better understanding of this difference, let us consider the definition of project again. A *project* is any activity that infers a complex and single one-time activity with a duration time (beginning and end) and cost (resources) constraints and that aims to achieve a definite result. A project can be described and defined by the performance result to be achieved and by time and cost constraints. This is illustrated in a broadly accepted way in Figure 1.3.

A project can always be described by its characteristics (i.e., its primary targets); however, it is also true that there could be tradeoffs among the primary project targets. For example, the budget can be cut by extending the time constraints and vice versa; the time constraints can be reduced if a lower quality of project result is to be achieved and vice versa. In the same way, the relation between the project result (including scope, quality, completeness, and so on) and the budget is similar. A clear understanding of the primary project targets is essential for the implementation of organizational strategy. Decisions concerning the project targets have to be made by the organization's strategic management or by the strategic level of the management. This is a principle to be followed even if the preparation was made at the project management level.

During the implementation of a project, the execution is characterized by a number of uncertainties and, as a corollary, risks related to the project result, duration time, and budget. Managers at project management level (i.e., in the role of managing project implementation) are responsible not only for the project's implementation but also for the achievement of the primary project targets. As for allocation of risks and responsibilities that the contributors take (i.e., the formulation of project strategy) there is a question of decision-making that should belong to the authority of the project manager.

The responsibility of strategic management does not come to an end with setting the strategic objectives and formulating the

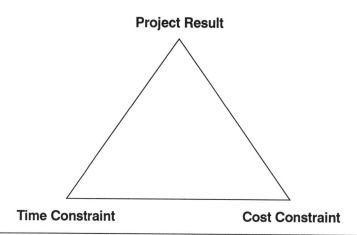

Project Result

Time Constraint **Cost Constraint**

**Figure 1.3   Characteristics Identifying a Project as Primary
Project Targets**

projects, which includes decision-making on the primary project targets. The environment of the organization may change considerably while the strategy and projects are being carried out; this may result in reformulation or serious modification of the strategy. All this can go together with the modification or sometimes with the cancellation of projects. Strategic management has to match the suitability of the projects under implementation and the actual organizational strategy. With an eye on the mentioned interrelations, Figure 1.4 exhibits a strategy formulation and project implementation model.

So far we have been more concerned with the interrelation between organizational strategy and projects than with strategic management and project management, respectively. Light has been shed on the place and role of project management in organizations. At the same time, we have referred to the fact that in spite of important similarities, project management represents an approach that is different from strategic management; it differs from operating management, as well. Based on some general principles, which are shown in Table 1.1, a comparison between strategic, project, and operating management is illustrated.

Grouping of Projects

An organization is bound, depending on the extent of the changes taking place at the organization, to simultaneously implement

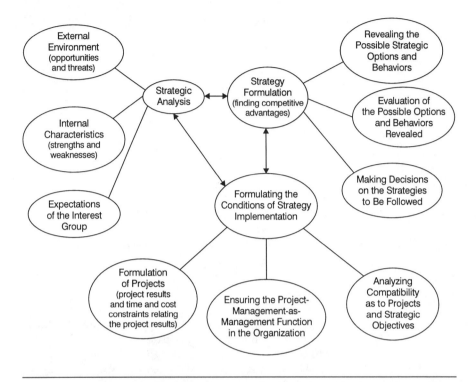

Figure 1.4   The Model of Strategy Formulation and Its Connection with Project Management

several strategic objectives and actions. Consequently, there are several projects undergoing implementation partly in parallel, partly overlapping, and partly in series. The characteristics, or the primary project targets, have been defined earlier. One of these is the project result to be achieved while implementing the project, which, being adjusted to the organizational strategy, enables a gradual implementation (project by project) of the organizational strategy.

The implementation of several strategic objectives present within an organization makes the achievement of several project results demanding. For example, the strategy's objectives may include innovation of a new product, creation of necessary production capacity, acquisition of market share, and, if necessary, modification of the company's organizational and ownership structures. It is evident that projects formulated in order to implement these strategic objectives are significantly different from each other with regard to both the activity content and the nature of the project result to be achieved. The existence of projects involving different activities and

Aspects of the Comparison	Strategic Management	Project Management	Operating Management
Time Horizon of Decision-Making	Long Term	Medium Term	Short Term
Influence on the Entire Organization	Decisive in Long Term	Decisive in Medium Term	Decisive in Short Term
Motivating Forces	The Likely Future Environment	The Primary Project Targets	Resources at Disposal and/or the Actual Market Situation
Nature of the Activity	Complex, Innovative	Complex, Innovative	Routine-like, Standardized
Continuity of Activity	Continuous	One Time, Recurring	Continuous
Scope of the Activity	The Entire Organization	The Entire Organization or More than One Single Functional Unit	A Single Functional Unit

Table 1.1   Management Functions Reflected in the Interrelation between Strategy and Projects

producing results of different natures enables the classification of projects necessary to be able to apply the methodological and technical means of project management more effectively and accurately. (These topics will be discussed in detail in later chapters of the book.) Projects can be categorized under the following headings: capital investment-engineering projects, research and development projects, and intellectual service projects.

Capital investment-engineering projects involve the realization of a new facility for producing products or services. If an already existing facility is rebuilt, refurbished, enlarged, or closed down, these also come under the same heading. For instance, an oil refinery, motorway, hospital, or database system could be included under this heading. It is characteristic of these projects that the desired project result can be described and defined by means of technical and/or performance parameters. Also characteristic of projects belonging to this category is that the most decisive resources during the implementation phase are material by nature, such as equipment, machines, different materials, and so on. The expected outcome of such projects can be modeled, but no prototype, in the real sense of the word, can be produced. However, experiences from the implementation or reconstruction of previous similar facilities, if there are any, and if such information is available, can be useful.

Research and development projects involve any project that results in:

■ a new product or new technology
■ improvement of an existing product or technology
■ manufacturing of a new product or introducing a new service
■ reduction in production costs
■ acquisition of new market share, and so on.

As with capital investment-engineering projects, it is characteristic of research and development projects that the project result can be defined quantitatively. In cases involving a new product or technology and improvement of an existing product or technology, the result can be mainly defined by technical parameters. At the same time, what becomes even more characteristic of this category is that, along with the material resources needed for the implementation of the project, human resources become more significant. In product-development projects, which also belong to this category, a prototype may be developed, while in the rest of the cases modeling or experience derived from previous similar projects can be useful.

Intellectual service projects are all those projects that result in new qualities of operating within the organization. Because the term is relatively new, neither in literature nor in practice is there a unanimously acknowledged name for this group of projects. One often runs across the terms, *management project* or *orgware project*; the latter refers to the transformation of the organization. The term, *change project*, also emerges, which confuses the mind since every project prompts some changes in the organization.

Modification of a company's organizational or ownership structures (e.g., privatization) or large-scale training or retraining of its members are examples of intellectual service projects. In many cases, the expected result of such projects cannot be directly or adequately quantified. Rather, the impact of the expected project result can be described. The efficiency of these projects can mainly be indirectly described, while the expected project result can be modeled. Experiences from previous similar projects can be of use. The human resource is the main resource for implementation of an intellectual service project.

As has been stated earlier, projects can be specified or identified by the likely result, the duration for the realization of the result, and the budget. These three characteristics are the primary targets of any project. The result of the project and its quality can be expanded by increasing time and cost constraints and vice versa, while time con-

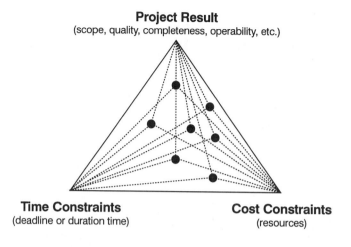

Project Result
(scope, quality, completeness, operability, etc.)

Time Constraints
(deadline or duration time)

Cost Constraints
(resources)

Figure 1.5   Diversity of Combinations of the Primary Project Targets

straints can be cut at the expense of costs and vice versa. The primary targets of a given project have to be adjusted to the organizational strategy all the time, which justifies that the project formation and decision-making regarding project options have to be made at the strategic level of management. In this way, a certain combination of result, cost, and duration time can be identified, which *guarantees* the adjustment of a single project to the strategy. The adjustment of project to project in an organization is also a decisive factor during strategy implementation, since a product-development project can often be accompanied by capital investment-engineering projects and marketing projects, or with projects that serve to train or retrain employees. The demand that a given project should adjust to the strategy may result in a number of combinations of the primary targets. This is illustrated in Figure 1.5, which was developed by means of Figure 1.3 and where the black points in the project triangle refer to the variety of the result-cost-time combination.

The number of possible combinations in practice is restricted by a valid and realistic strategy. It is not rare, however, to come across a number of projects where one of the primary targets—namely the duration time or the project deadline—is not flexible and cannot be changed. These projects, beyond the previous classification, can be referred to as event-like projects. The Olympic Games or a world exhibition are good examples of this type of project. Another characteristic of these projects is that they are extremely complex and often contain some individual subprojects, such as capital investment-engineering projects, research and development projects, and intellectual service projects. That is why these large projects are often referred to as super-projects or megaprojects. The responsibility of strategic management is twofold in these projects: first, the formation of the megaproject, which involves the given event; and, second, the further utilization of the leftover project results, such as the facilities and organizations.

Beyond the classification of the projects we have dealt with above, one can find in the literature another classification, which is based on whether the implementation of the project result is brought about by external contributors or basically by the internal resources of the client. In this respect, *external* and *internal projects* can be identified. This classification is also very important to efficient project management; thus, it is significant to effective strategy implementation, as well. In general, the majority of capital investment-engineering projects are external; a significant majority of research and development projects are internal; and intellectual service projects are partly external and partly internal.

So far, whether it has been declared or not, projects innovative by nature have been mentioned. It should be noted, however, that project management—both its methodological and technical aspects—can be used for the implementation of strategies involving projects that are different by nature than the ones we have examined. For example, organizational strategy, in order to fight a crisis or wind up a bankruptcy, besides the innovative actions involves projects such as withdrawal from a market, winding up certain activities, and so forth. Also characteristic to these projects is that they involve one-time complex activities that aim toward implementing previously well-defined targets. Furthermore, the time and cost constraints of these targets are given; thus, they are also projects.

Chapter Two

The Project Cycle and
Inherent Characteristics of the
Project Process

C HAPTER 1 WAS concerned with the variety of projects and identifying criteria for their classification. In order to be able to
handle the implementation of various projects, first of all from the
point of view of methodology, the need for a conceptual framework
arises. This framework is nothing other than the project cycle, and
it presents project implementation as a strategy-oriented workflow.
In accordance with the project cycle itself, as well as with the introduction of the different activity phases, the framework does not
describe the workflow processes in detail. Instead, it concentrates on
the strategic determination of the decision points, which not only
connect but also separate the different activities in the cycle.

This chapter offers a comprehensive picture of the uncertainties
and interdependence that form the basis for the majority of
decision-making approaches and methodological backgrounds
applicable in project management. Both interdependence and
uncertainty are inherent characteristics in project implementation.
Their importance in decision-making methodology can be easily
recognized, both in the case of project strategy formulation and
when different organizational forms are considered. Their importance also shines through when project time scheduling and risk
analyses are performed.

The Capital Investment-Engineering Project Cycle

Projects that belong to the group of capital investment-engineering
projects, especially those that result in the creation of new facilities,

can be regarded as classical cases of project management. A capital investment-engineering project comprises a series of activities from the emergence of a demand for a facility triggered by the organizational strategy up to the start-up of the facility.

Implementation of new facilities as projects has a several-hundred-year history; based on some historic examples—e.g., Great Pyramids, Great Wall of China, and so on—there could be a several-thousand-year history. What contradicts this idea is that under the special socioeconomic circumstances of the age, only the project result to be achieved and the strategy that brought it into being—mainly without definite time and cost constraints—was set.

In spite of inevitable changes, methods and techniques applied in this field have become so well established that sometimes one should refer to them as *standards*. Solutions and processes in traditional practice served as models for the implementation of research and development projects and intellectual service projects. The latter have become more and more decisive, with regard to their number and strategic significance, in the second half of the Twentieth Century.

The implementation of a capital investment-engineering project implies a series of steps, including the necessary decisions that are built upon each other. These procedures make a good starting point for managing the implementation of other kinds of projects, as well.

Last but not least, the majority of capital investment-engineering projects are external projects. This fact, while keeping in mind the previous two, makes the necessity of the appropriate formulation of project strategy self-evident. (Project strategy includes the allocation of risks and responsibilities that are associated with the project result to be achieved, and risks and responsibilities that are associated with the time and cost constraints of the project implementation.) From what has been described, it is clear that the introduction of a general model of the capital investment-engineering project cycle takes precedence; the generic model of the project cycle will be introduced subsequently.

The capital investment-engineering project cycle is nothing other than the framework of the strategic-oriented approach of the investment process. It presents the implementation process of capital investment-engineering projects in such a way that basic (critical) decision points separate the different phases of the workflow (preparation, awarding, implementation, and postevaluation). As can be seen in Figure 2.1 and Figure 2.2, the generic model of the project cycle, the capital-investment project cycle is literally a cycle.

Organizational strategy is at the center of the process. In other words, the strategic objectives and actions comprise the core; their realization makes the implementation of a facility necessary. At the same time, the process represented by the cycle returns to the

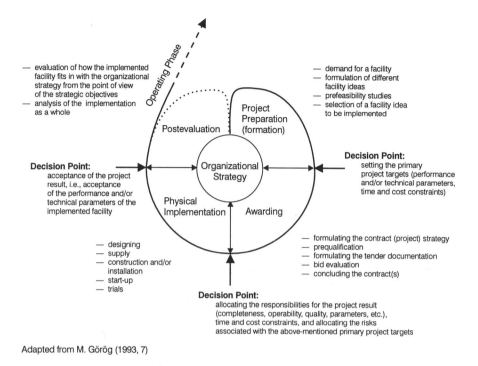

Adapted from M. Görög (1993, 7)

Figure 2.1   The Basic Model of the Capital Investment-Engineering Project Cycle

strategy in the last phase of the activity flow. While the cycle goes on, the monitoring of and matching with the actual organizational strategy become necessary, especially preceding the decision points.

Project preparation is the first phase of the activities in the capital investment-engineering project cycle. This activity phase comes through in overlap between the functions of strategic management and project management. The demand for a new facility is motivated by the necessity to achieve the strategic objectives, and it becomes defined by setting the results of different project ideas. The perception of the reciprocity of the strategic and project management functions plays an extremely important role in the first phase of activities in the cycle. The different technologies that can be applied—the equipment that makes these technologies work, the different buildings that provide a home for the equipment, and the variety of raw materials, not to mention variations caused by the scale or the site—create in a given case a number of different facility options.

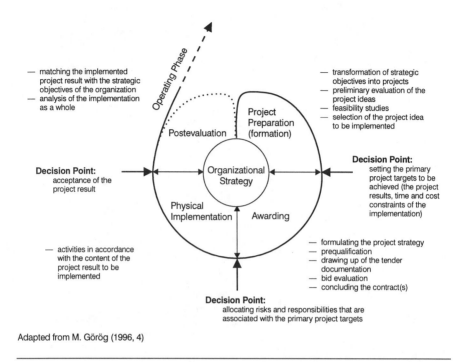

— matching the implemented project result with the strategic objectives of the organization
— analysis of the implementation as a whole

Operating Phase

Postevaluation

Project Preparation (formation)

Organizational Strategy

Physical Implementation

Awarding

— transformation of strategic objectives into projects
— preliminary evaluation of the project ideas
— feasibility studies
— selection of the project idea to be implemented

Decision Point:
acceptance of the project result

Decision Point:
setting the primary project targets to be achieved (the project results, time and cost constraints of the implementation)

— activities in accordance with the content of the project result to be implemented

— formulating the project strategy
— prequalification
— drawing up of the tender documentation
— bid evaluation
— concluding the contract(s)

Decision Point:
allocating risks and responsibilities that are associated with the primary project targets

Adapted from M. Görög (1996, 4)

Figure 2.2   The Generic Model of the Project Cycle

Out of the great number of possible options, prefeasibility studies about the implementation lay the foundation for the selection of those facility options that can be implemented in the given circumstances. Further on, based on detailed feasibility studies, the most suitable option for achieving the strategic objectives can be identified.

Since the expected result of capital investment-engineering projects can be defined in a quantitative way, the likely contribution of their implementation to the actual strategic objectives can also be calculated. Similarly, it is also true—as far as capital investment-engineering projects are concerned, with the exception of some especially complicated refurbishment projects—that the work process producing the project result (the facility) can be described and defined in a quantitative way, too.

If there are realistic and stable strategic objectives, the need for matching the actual state of the project implementation with the strategic objectives at the further decision points becomes less significant but not negligible.

The activities of the awarding phase concentrate on the strategy of the project implementation in the sense that allocation of the responsibilities and risks that are associated with the physical implementation phase is formulated during this phase. In capital investment-engineering projects, the allocation of risk and responsibilities is first concerned with operability, completeness, and technical and/or performance parameters—i.e., the project result to be implemented—and later with the duration time and costs of implementation. To put it differently, the allocation is brought forth based partly on the type of contract and partly on the financial settlement (see Chapters 5 and 6). If the organizational strategy is realistic and stable, matching of the outcome of the decision made on project strategy with the organizational strategy objectives could become routine. Under these circumstances, taking into consideration the outcomes of the risk analyses, the project strategy can be properly formulated, based on the project profile and the client profile. Otherwise, when the organizational strategy is undergoing changes, the previously mentioned matching may have a critical effect on the project implementation strategy.

If the organizational strategy is basically fixed, but the details are not yet certain, the result may be a project or contract strategy—e.g., a traditional type of contract and a cost-based financial settlement—that otherwise would contradict the relevant characteristic values of the project profile and the client profile. If meanwhile the organizational strategy undergoes changes, as in the preparation phase, it may result in the cancellation of the project. As far as the project profile is concerned in the concrete value of the character as to the *scope, performance and technical parameters of the facility* can demonstrate the changing character of the organizational strategy (see Chapter 6).

The physical implementation of the facility prompts the third phase of the capital investment-engineering project cycle when, as a result of the different technical workflows, the project result is brought into being. In this phase, the project strategy directly exerts an impact on the achievement of the primary project targets. If the implemented primary project targets are not reflected in the objectives of the organizational strategy, the reasons for the problem must be found in the project/contract strategy. This interrelation leads to the postevaluation phase.

Postevaluation, the last phase of the project cycle, takes place when the success of the project implementation can be evaluated, based partly on the analysis of the entire implementation process and partly on how the organization achieved its goals and objectives with the help of the project in question. The project success, in the broader sense of the word, can be assessed here, also taking into consideration the behavior of the different interest groups in connection with the project.

The Generic Model of the Project Cycle

Literature on the project cycle is concerned mainly with describing the activities in the individual phases of the cycle. Yet, attention given to capital investment-engineering projects also remains in the forefront.

Less attention is given to showing the essential interrelations than to depicting the cycle. Generally speaking, literature describes two basic approaches to depicting the project cycle. In one frequently applied illustration, the phases of the project cycle are placed linearly one after the other above a time axis, an approach used, for example by D. I. Cleland (1994) and P. A. Thompson (1981). The other less frequently used illustration of the project cycle is the hierarchic illustration, and its logic derives from the system analysis. The hierarchic illustration is based on the logical interrelation of the phases and the activities that they imply; A. Walker uses this kind of depiction (1989). Without giving a more detailed analysis, it will be sufficient here to call attention to the fact that this illustration can be explained, but at the same time it is not suitable for underlining the essential strategic determination of projects. It is a wonder that Cleland, a pioneer in the recognition of strategy-oriented project management has not undertaken to illustrate it in the project cycle.

The project cycle can be depicted as a circle hub; interpreted in this way, the project activities are placed in a conceptual frame that enhances exploration of the essential process interrelations. At the same time, both from the aspects of the work process and the interrelations between projects and strategic objectives, the cycle reveals the critical decision points. The critical decision points then, in turn, at the same time create the border elements of the activity phases in the cycle. This approach is reflected in Figure 2.2. It is remarkable that L. G. Goodman and R. N. Love use a similar approach (1980). Even if their illustration applies only to the capital investment-engineering projects, they illustrate the project cycle in a more or less similar way.

To gain a better understanding of the significance of the project cycle that can be attributed to this approach, the reader has to go back to the discussion on project typology in Chapter 1 under Grouping of Projects.

Capital investment-engineering projects have many advantageous characteristics from the point of view of definition. The facility, which is the result of the project, can be defined with the help of technical and performance parameters and standards. The workflow can also be described in a quantitative way. These characteristics of the capital investment-engineering projects can indeed be traced back to similar characteristics of the strategic objectives and actions that call them into being. If the project is properly implemented, the new facility is nearly automatically adjustable to the daily operation of the organization, since the creation of the project result is also measurable in a quantitative way. It can be seen how these circumstances—taking the workflow and including the phases of the project cycle as a basis—shape the mutual relation between strategy and project when decisions are made.

The set and expected result of research and development projects can also be defined more or less in a quantitative way, similarly to the strategic objectives and actions to be achieved by these projects. This is less expected from the workflow, which brings about the project result because of the relative novelty of the activity. As a corollary, during the implementation of the project, a number of unforeseeable opportunities for ramification present themselves, which increase the number of those decisions that are described in Figure 2.2 as either critical or basic and which therefore cannot be always and exactly fixed numerically.

Developing new technical solutions (product, technology) may generate a number of emergency situations when decisions have to be made during implementation. Looking at it in another way, it means that there are serious uncertainties associated with the workflow, while achievement of the project result or the strategic objectives is at stake.

The proper quantification of intellectual service projects is even more uncertain. The problem of attempting to produce an exact project definition can have an impact not only on the workflow that brings about the project result but also on the result itself. In most cases, these projects cannot be satisfactorily quantified; at best, only the likely effects during the operation phase of the project result can be described. It can be perceived, however, in the case of a project that as a result produces a new organizational structure for the company; one has to keep in mind that putting the project result into operation cannot be considered as a single action either.

It has to be emphasized that when the different types of projects are examined, the observations described above are true in general, but within the general characteristics the actual observations may vary from project to project.

The more difficult it is to determine the expected project result in a quantitative way—or, the more difficult it is to quantify the outcome of the project—the more likely it is that a result other than that originally desired might occur. Similarly, if the approach to project management is not strategically oriented, then there is a danger of misconception in the project formation phase and of identification of inappropriate targets during the project implementation stage.

Taking into consideration these two issues, one can come to the conclusion—justified by practice a number of times—that the less quantifiable a project is, the more important it is in project management to have a strategic-oriented approach that encompasses project implementation as a whole. The illustration of the project cycle applied here draws attention to the absolute necessity of this approach. While keeping an eye on this approach, the most important elements of the project phases will be revealed in brief, based on the generic model of the project cycle.

The cycle breaks the entire project implementation into the following main activity phases:

- project formation
- awarding
- implementation
- postevaluation.

These phases are set apart by three critical decision points. The cycle takes its starting point in the first phase from the strategic objectives (actions), and in the last phase it comes to the end of its life at the same point.

During the project formation phase, strategic determination is still more or less obvious. From this, we see that the most remarkable activity of the phase is the preparation of feasibility studies concerning the implementation of different viable project options, since this is the activity that results in a decision regarding which of the project options will be selected and implemented. Thus, this activity leads directly to the first critical decision point. In well-quantifiable projects, the activity can be carried out in an exact way, and the project option selected for implementation can be defined in the same manner. When a project cannot be quantified, the project formation activities become a lot more difficult; therefore, a need for detailed feasibility studies increases in importance. Under these circumstances, detailed feasibility studies that explore the likely effects of the operating phase of the project result can increase the quantifiable nature of the project and contribute to a more exact specification of the option to be implemented. Otherwise, they can impede the project implementation and divert from the primary targets to be achieved.

The strategy of implementation—i.e., the project strategy or contract strategy—is in essence refined during the awarding phase. Further activities of this phase are determined by the project strategy; thus, implementation strategy can be considered as most important in this phase. As a result of the decision made at the critical decision point at the end of the phase, the concrete forms and means of allocation of risks and responsibilities that are associated with the expected result (completeness, quality, operability) are refined. Further the allocation of those risks and responsibilities that are associated with the entire duration time and the cost constraint of the implementation are concerned. In this respect, both experience and theoretical considerations draw attention to two important facts.

First, when the strategic objectives undergo changes in the course of the project-awarding phase or when the strategy concerning the details is not fully developed, reaching the decision point that ends the phase and matching the strategic objectives and the primary project targets can be critically important. This can have an effect not only on the project result achieved during the implementation, but also on the extent of achievement of the strategic objectives realized by the project.

The second fact to be emphasized is also concerned with the extent of the quantifiable nature of projects. The less quantifiable a project result, the less successfully activities of the awarding phase can be carried out. Thus, before final decisions are made, the more important it is to match the strategic objectives with the expected project result.

In both of the above-mentioned cases, the explanation derives from the same root. The awarding phase in the project cycle is the time when, coming to the critical decision point, the commitment of the resources necessary for the implementation takes place. In external projects, this occurs in the form of contracts that can be enforced by law. Before getting to this decision point, the project can be modified or cancelled with relatively small losses.

The activities carried out during implementation are determined by the specific workflow needed to achieve the project result. With well-quantifiable projects, given that the strategic objectives do not change, fewer strategic considerations have to be accommodated. However, when a project is not so well quantifiable, matching the strategic objectives with the actual state of the project implementation gains more importance. Even a research and development project can involve a number of possibilities for ramifications that were not foreseeable during project preparation. Each of the possible ramifications implies a need to make a decision. (What is essential here is that the decisions that end the first phase of the cycle, as far as certain details are concerned, are shifted to the implementation phase.) In such a case, a project result in accordance with the strategy is only likely if all of the possibilities arising at a certain branch are matched with the strategic objectives. Experience proves that if the opposite happens, the contributors may successfully influence the decisions in accordance with their own interests (usual solutions, financial, or other advantages); i.e., they can draw the project result away from the client's strategy.

The decision-making point that ends this phase applies to the acceptance of the project result. In all practicality, this is the last opportunity for rejection of the project due to inadequate performance of the contributors or implementation that was not in accordance with the primary project targets.

Once the project result is accepted, it is integrated into the organization's daily operations. The last phase, postevaluation, can begin with examining the entire project implementation, making it part of the project management learning process, while evaluating the operating project result. Evaluating the operating project result is important in order to assess whether the strategic objectives are fulfilled by the implemented project result. Depending on the nature of the strategic objectives, the analysis can be conducted in a short period of time; in other cases, it can be carried out only over a long time period and is often based on probability calculations.

The presented generic model of the project cycle is suitable for drawing attention to the strategic determination of projects. This determination is almost visible in the first and last phases of the project cycle, but successful project management cannot do without this approach either in the award phase or during implementation. It has to be noted here that it rather frequently happens that project ideas occur to people who work at an organization's operating level, far from top management. The presented model of the project cycle does not contain this aspect. We cannot omit either that some of the above-mentioned project ideas may modify organizational strategy.

We should also note that it is not wise to make decisions during the project cycle without performing a preliminary analysis of the likely risks. Risks in some form are almost always present in every activity phase of the project cycle. Evaluating the likely effects of risks can significantly modify the decision to be made. Experience underlines the fact that considering risks before making decisions at the first two critical decision points of the project cycle is of great importance.

The Inherent Characteristics of Project Implementation

The characteristics of a given project can be found in the inherent characteristics of the project and in its implementation. Every project has two basic characteristics: different sorts of interdependence and different kinds of uncertainty accompany them. One of the Tavistock Institute's studies states that uncertainty and interdependence are twin brothers in the process of implementing a facility (1966). Although this statement applies to capital investment-engineering projects, considerable examples in the field of research and development and in intellectual service projects prove that uncertainty and interdependence are inherent characteristics of all of the different types of projects. It is frequently observed that uncertainty and interdependence mutually influence each other. For example, in cases where more uncertainty factors concerning the project result are present at the same time, more complex interdependence is characteristic of the workflow bringing about the project result. Experiences also prove that when the project implementation is characterized by more complex interdependence, it can frequently be explained by the great extent of novelty (as one of the significant sources of uncertainty) of the operating process of the project result, and so forth.

The question is whether the claim that uncertainty and interdependence are the inherent characteristics of projects can be explained. For the sake of better understanding, one should utilize Table 2.1 to compare the characteristics of a typical operating-management activity (managing industrial mass production) and a typical project-implementation process (capital investment-engineering project).

The characteristics shown in Table 2.1 gain significance from the point of view of uncertainty, and the following of them are to be emphasized.

- The end product of project implementation, the project result, can rarely be practically standardized; thus, in the majority of cases, it can be considered unique.
- Sale and purchase in every case precede not only implementation of the project result but the beginning of the implementation, as well.

Uncertainty, after all, can be interpreted as the source of risks in implementation. Uncertainty can be varied in different types of projects, but even within the same group of different projects can be diverse. As an *aide mémoire*, a list of the most important project-specific groups of uncertainties present in the implementation phase of projects would include:

- novelty and the extent of novelty of the operating process of the project result
- definition of the project scope and the extent of project formation, as to details
- novelty and the extent of novelty of the workflow, which brings about the project result
- stability and the extent of stability as to the socioeconomic environment, especially the legal environment
- inflation and its extent (or its acceleration) during the course of the implementation phase.

When capital investment-engineering projects are considered, another very important uncertainty factor is site investigation. First, the geological, hydrological, meteorological, and other characteristics, as well as the possibility of existing underground facilities, are assessed.

Industrial Mass Production	Project Implementation (capital investment-engineering project)
Production of the same products takes place in a factory, practically in unchanging conditions during a certain period of time.	Sites of the implementation of the facilities vary facility to facility.
Products are standardized.	The project result in its entirety, i.e., the facility, is not standardized even if it consists of many standardized elements.
Production takes precedence over selling and buying.	Selling and buying take precedence over the implementation of the facility.
Manufacturing of the products is initiated by the manufacturer.	Demand for the facility is initiated by the buyer, i.e., the client.
Substitution of products is available in a wide range; thus, buyers can choose based on different considerations. Apart from the so-called prestige consuming, prices play a decisive role.	Possibilities of substitution are more narrow while prices are decisive, but not the only (and not always the most decisive) consideration as to the choice.

Table 2.1   Basic Characteristics of Different Management Activities

Interdependence implies the mutual interrelations of the operating process of a system; i.e., it implies how operability of the single processes depends on each other. At a lower level, it indicates the same interrelation among the elements of the system that make the functions operable and, at the same time, the complexity and scale relations of the elements.

Different types of interdependence can be arranged according to their complexity, as follows.

- Workflow interdependence, which can be:
  - pooled
  - sequential (simple or overlapping)
  - reciprocal.
- Process interdependence, which characterizes the operating functions of the project result.
- Scale interdependence, which indicates the complexity of the project result and the diversity of the functions provided by it on the one hand, while on the other indicating the economies of scale.

With regard to the above, it should be noted that interdependence of a certain complexity always involves interdependence of less complexity.

Pooled interdependence occurs in a given work process when certain activities rely as a starting point on the outcome of a previously completed activity. In this way, the faulty or correct outcome of certain activities exerts an impact on the quality of those tasks that are based on them. Examples of this phenomenon are easily observed when the interrelationship between some parts of the feasibility studies is considered.

The main point concerning sequential interdependence is that certain activities cannot be started as long as the fulfillment of other preceding activities are not completed; this is simple sequentiality. When partial fulfillment of a preceding activity allows the beginning of fulfillment of a succeeding activity, it is referred to as overlapping sequentiality.

Reciprocal interdependence takes place when a task to be implemented has more than one contributor who are in different roles with regard to their contributions to the task in question. The task itself is passed back and forth among the contributors until it is completed. The feasibility studies also provide good examples of this phenomenon.

Process interdependence of the operating project result means the way in which some parts of the entire process, from the point of view of their operability, influence each other. A number of examples can be found in the chemical and food industry where operability of a certain part of the entire process—i.e., a part of a certain process technology—depends on the operability of the preceding process(es). At the same time, some sectors of the machine industry show the opposite phenomenon, since some parts of the manufacturing process, concerning their operability, do not depend on each other.

In order to understand the essence of scale interdependence, it is useful for one to think about the difference between an international airport—a very complex facility providing a great number of functions—and a petrol station, which provides only a few. Beyond the economies of scale, in the first place, interdependence relates to the complexity of the project result to be implemented.

It should be noted that some types of interdependence, such as workflow, are characteristic of every activity. In this respect, the specific nature of project implementation is that the presence of complex interdependence is overwhelmingly characteristic of it, as opposed to the significantly simpler interdependence of daily routine operations of an organization.

Chapter Three

Project Formation

I N THIS CHAPTER, the authors present a set of tools for project formation that can be generally applied to any project, which is methodologically coherent, offering a possibility for strategy-oriented project management, as well. This approach is based on the project structure plans.

In every case while implementing the project, the given organization carries out its strategic objectives, and the project result becomes part of the operating function of the organization. This way, it becomes clear that the first step in realizing the strategy is nothing less than a transformation of strategic objectives into projects. This process, the formation of the project, has to be based on the functions to be performed by the expected project result, and it necessitates that the function structure of the project be planned. During project implementation, however, the functions themselves are not implemented; the function vehicles—i.e., those means that make the individual functions operable—are implemented. This is what justifies planning the structure of the function vehicles. Also, last but not least, the clear and full-scale definition of the project itself—the completeness of the transformation of strategic objectives into a project—also necessitates expanding the structure of those activities that accomplish the structure of function vehicles, or the expected project result.

Considering that these project structures simultaneously result in an integrated approach to project structure plans, the latter, based on the results gained analyzing the structure plans, creates the practical basis for strategic-oriented project management. The approach of project formation as outlined here and the formation of the most fundamental tools and considerations of strategic-oriented project management have been worked out partly as the result of the generalization of experience and partly based on logical consistency.

The Structures of Operating Functions and Function Vehicles

In the first chapter, projects were expounded in terms of strategic goals and objectives and then finally in strategic actions, which can be found at the lower level of the hierarchically built system of strategy conception. The same approach was continued in Chapter 2 through the strategically oriented depiction of the project cycle, while the immanent characteristics of projects were emphasized. The basic condition of implementation, its practicability, lies in the fact that all of the different strategic actions have to be transformed into projects. As a result, several project options come into being, and, later, analysis of the feasibility of the options is possible. Then, based on the analysis result, the project options can be ranked, allowing selection of the option to be implemented possible. (However, feasibility studies are not discussed in this book.)

While strategic objectives and actions are converted into projects, or rather as the result of this, the scope of the project is shaped. The following important factors have an effect on the scope of the project:

- number and content (characters) of the functions, which have to be provided by the project result during its operating phase
- scope (size or capacity) of the individual functions
- complexity, characters, and so on of the *means* (i.e., function vehicles) that realize operability of the individual functions.

The scope of the functions to be provided has without any doubt a serious impact on the project scope although the functions' values are influenced by a number of factors, such as technological and market constraints and user demand. These factors act as forces and from time to time as real constraints during the conception of strategic objectives, rather than as independent variables of strategy setting. From a different aspect, the scope of functions is closely related to different disciplines. Producing a set of rules that would provide such a guideline, and which would apply to each project, is nearly impossible; if it is possible, it remains too general. In this chapter, attention will be drawn to the operating functions to be provided and the means and elements that realize the operability of the functions.

Strategic objectives are achieved by means of projects, and the completed project results are integrated into the operating functions of the organization. Thus, project results have to provide specific functions—services, technological processes, information forwarding. In this way, the outlined future state or the vision to be achieved is brought about in the organization itself. The function structure of an individual project can be outlined, based on the actions of the organizational strategy and considering the specified project result to be achieved.

The function structure is a hierarchically built system, and one can find at the top the expected project result in its entirety, or the strategic objective to be achieved. Under this, there are the bigger groups of functions, known as subfunctions. Obviously, these subfunctions fall underneath the main function groups, since they are elements of them. This breaking down can be carried to the level of the *elementary functions*, meaning the smallest part of a function to which a specifiable element of the function vehicles can be identified.

In order to get a clear-cut picture of the function structure, let us take an example well known in everyday life: a filling station. The main functions of an average filling station during its operating phase could be listed as follows:

- safe storage of various fuels
- comfortable service for drivers filling vehicles
- car wash
- sale of different commodities.

Within the main function groups, there are some subfunctions; e.g., the sale of the different commodities may include the following:

- storage of car-care commodities
- storage of spare parts
- storage of foodstuffs
- making invoices
- safe storage of cash.

The elementary functions for the subfunction, storage of foodstuffs, could be:

- gondola storage
- refrigerator storage.

Figure 3.1 presents the function structure for the filling station. In order to avoid confusion, this structure is broken down to the level of subfunctions only.

Project management literature, including international literature, is not really concerned with function structure. The reason is that the strategic-oriented approach to project management cannot at present be considered as a generally accepted approach. Both academics and professionals have not realized that organizational strategy is carried out in the form of a series of projects to be implemented. It is the function structure that really connects strategic management with project management, ensuring continuity between them. At the same time, working out the function structure is also such a serious profession-based task that description and exploration of some general rules that would give guidance is rather difficult.

One of the advantages gained by creating a function structure is the possibility that the formation of different project options could

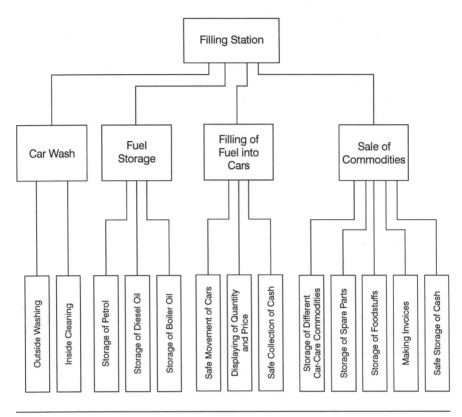

Figure 3.1   The Structure of the Operating Functions

result in operable systems. Working out the function structure aims in this direction, but the function analysis that can be made based on the structure contributes considerably more toward it. Another advantage is that while working on such an analysis, the process interdependence can be basically explored. In other words, one can explore how the single functions are interrelated during the operation phase. Consequently, it can be specified which functions operate independently of each other and which mutually depend upon each other, avoiding the possibility of an incomplete project result, from the point of view of strategic objectives by function. All in all, those functions that are necessary but which have not been counted can be minimized. The more complex the expected project result is and the less it can be defined in a quantitative way, the more likely that incompleteness will occur.

A function structure also makes a good starting point for preparation of feasibility studies. Preparation for the expected project result can be more accurate, which is very important in order to achieve the strategic objectives, when a function analysis based on the function structure is made. Based on this function analysis, the structure of the function vehicles can be expanded. Scope formation of the desired project result nears completion in this manner, which is why the structure of function vehicles also is stressed in this chapter.

Generally speaking, a function vehicle can be any element of the project result (hardware, software, or orgware, for example) that enables function elements or functions to be simultaneously or consecutively set and kept going. For example, in a hotel, the function vehicles would include the building and all of the facilities, furniture, parts (rooms, restaurants, swimming pools, hairdresser's shop, and so on) inside the building, and the parking place and so forth outside the building. The organizational structure with its appropriate information system and so on has to be considered as a function vehicle, as well, when the project aims toward transformation of the organizational structure. With the help of the structure of the function vehicles, one can get an answer to the question: What sets and keeps the different functions that have to be provided by the project result going? During the project implementation, the functions to be provided are not directly carried out. Instead the means that provide the function vehicles are created, or existing elements of possible function vehicles are arranged in a combination ensuring the operability of the project result.

One should bear in mind that the following factors could have effect on the structure of the possible function vehicles:

- environmental conditions of operation, such as legal forces, pressure and temperature, and so forth
- the outcomes of a value analysis, especially in the case of a tangible project result.

The structure of the function vehicles is compiled, based on the function structure, but it is not necessarily its own reflection. Figure 3.2 illustrates the structure of function vehicles of the previously mentioned filling station.

The structure of the function vehicles is also hierarchically built, and one can find on the top the project result as the entity to be implemented. This is followed by the main groups of function vehicles, which realize the first-line main function groups of the function structure. These can be further broken down if necessary to the level of the elementary function vehicles. The smallest elements of the function vehicles, which have the capability of making a part of a function operate, can be called elementary function vehicles.

Although Figure 3.2 depicts the structure in a simple way without providing a detailed picture of the structure of the function vehicles in the facility, which was implemented as a result of the project, it is

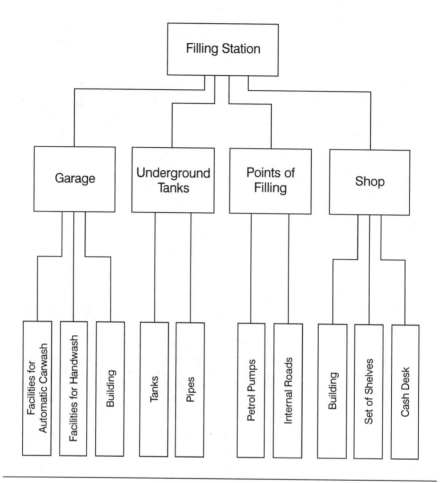

Figure 3.2   The Structure of the Function Vehicles

clear that certain functions (e.g., payment for fuel and commodities) can be brought into being through one and the same function vehicle. At the same time, the service station and the shop can be placed in the same building complex.

The structure of the function vehicles is set during project implementation; consequently, the project result can fulfill the planned functions during the operating phase. While working out the structure of the function vehicles based on the function structure, the project result to be implemented can be defined; thus, it is possible to describe and specify the content or scope of the project. As a corollary, anything that does not belong to the structure of the function vehicles cannot be considered as part of the project result.

In this way, a project can always be marked off from its environment; i.e., the scope of the project becomes clear while bearing in mind the scope of the single functions to be provided. The specification of a project scope as mentioned above provides the basis for an effective project implementation and for project success.

Obviously, the degree of quantifiability involved in defining the expected project result will largely depend on the exact nature of the project. Nevertheless, it could be stated, based on experiences, that expanding the structure of the function vehicles will contribute considerably to a more correct project definition, even in the course of feasibility studies. As a corollary, decision-making on the project options will also be more accurate. It can be said that due to working out the structure of the function vehicles, the advantages and possibilities listed in connection with the function structure can be augmented.

It is exceptional for an organization to have only one project; however, in this case, the project formation regards only one project. It is far more common, with regard to the diversity of strategic objectives, for the implementation of several projects, which are connected in one way or another with each other, to occur simultaneously in an organization. This phenomenon leads to the need to mark off projects. When, based on the strategic objectives of an organization, such actions are defined—for example, development of a new product, creation of production facilities, introducing the product into the market, and so on—one has to know where and when one project ends and the other starts. Otherwise, overlapping can occur, and important elements can be inadvertently omitted from both of the interrelated projects. In order to avoid this situation, both the function and function vehicles' structures can be used to define the scope of the project or to determine when a given project ends.

Naturally, specifying the beginning and end of a project with regard to project scope is important even when those projects are not interconnected. We shall examine this question from another point of view under Implications of an Integrated Approach to Project Structures later in this chapter. Yet, before proceeding with an explanation of project structure plans, it seems necessary to make three remarks in order for the applicability of the project structure plans in compliance with reality to be clear.

One of the remarks draws attention to the fact that the function and the function vehicles' structures cannot always be elaborated in the detailed way necessary during the first phase of the project cycle. Basically, there are two reasons for this. It is partly due to the incompletely outlined organizational strategy and the decision-making potential in the organization pertaining to the project, which is more or less interrelated with the incomplete organizational strategy. It also is due in part to the degree of quantifiability of the project.

Obviously, the less quantifiable a project is, the more it can be expected that only the first-line breakdown of the project structures can be detailed, especially in the case of the function vehicles' structure. It is plain that these circumstances will influence both the project plans (discussed in Chapter 4) and project strategy decision-making (discussed in Chapter 6).

In such a case, one has to face that certain elements of the decision-making process will shift into the implementation phase in accordance with possible ramifications, and acknowledge the fact that the detailed structure plan of the function vehicles can be shaped only gradually during the implementation phase. Many novel R&D projects are cases in point where a lot of decisions regarding details should be made during project implementation. In order to achieve the strategic objectives, it is worth trying to refine the structure of the functions even down to the details so that it precedes the formulation of the function vehicles' structure. It is not surprising that in most instances cost-based financial settlement is applied when referring to project strategy. The wise client will set a limit on the costs spent by the contributors in accordance with a detailed structure plan of the function vehicles, one that can be implemented in a realistic manner. It is also wise during the implementation, when decisions are made concerning ramifications and how to proceed with the project, to set the amount of the likely costs that can be spent before arriving at the next decision point.

The second remark is related to the appearance of the project result. The result of a considerable number of the projects is tangible, while a smaller number of projects has no significant material result at all; i.e., the project result is intangible by its nature (a conference, for example). In this case, it makes more sense—first of all, based on practical considerations—to speak about goal structure instead of function structure. Instead of the structure of function vehicles, it makes more sense to focus on the structure of means that will ensure achievement of the project goals. Experience shows that in some cases when the project result is intangible, it is sufficient to formulate only the goal structure. This is so, however, only if one can ensure that it leads to the right activity structure. (See the next section on activity structures.) Concerning its form of explanation, the goal structure corresponds with the function structure, while the structure of the means ensuring achievement of the project goals corresponds with the structure of the function vehicles.

Last but not least, it should be noted, in connection with both function structure and function vehicle structure, that at the top of their hierarchies the project result as a whole could be replaced in many cases by the strategic objective to be achieved.

Activity Structures

The marking off of the project result scope is possible with the help of the function vehicles' structure based on the function structure. In this way, regarding the project result, one of the primary project targets is defined, which implies that, from the point of view of the project content, the conversion of the strategic actions into projects could take place. During project implementation, the need for working out the structure of those activities that bring about the structure of the function vehicles arises. This, as a starting point, makes it possible to complete defining the primary project targets, i.e., refining time and cost constraints of implementing the desired project result.

The activity structure concentrates on the activities of the implementation phase of the project cycle, since in this phase those activities that directly realize the implementation of the function vehicles come to the forefront. Similar to the two structures discussed earlier, the activity structure is also a hierarchically built system where one can find the project result in its complexity and entirety at the top. Under it come those bigger activity packages; their formation is based on a criterion decided in advance. These points of view, i.e., the criteria, resulting in the first-line breakdown of the activities can be different, depending in part on the nature of the project. Considering the purpose or use, the applicable breakdown criteria generally used include the following:

- professional content of the activities
- first-line breakdown in the structure of the function vehicles
- first-line breakdown applied in the function structure
- geographical locations of the implementation
- contributing (external and/or in-house) organizations
- phases of the project cycle.

According to one of the criteria mentioned, a further breakdown of the activity groups implies that they should be broken down to smaller tasks, which can be further broken down to the level of the elementary activities. Elementary activities are those smallest activity units in which the necessary resources for fulfillment can be identified while the fulfillment itself can be measured. Figure 3.3 presents the activity structure for the implementation (only the implementation phase itself) of a chalet based on a first-line breakdown of the activities, which is in accordance with the professional content of the project activities.

Regardless of the criterion applied toward elaborating the first-line breakdown of the project activities, the result in every case is a listing of those activities that are considered necessary for implementing the project. Neglecting some of the activities can have serious consequences when, for example, a traditional type of contract is applied during the project strategy. In this case, it is the client who takes responsibility for the completeness of the project result and bears the risks, as well.

Experience shows that the more detailed the activity structure is, the less possible that it neglects any of the activities. Experience also justifies that a too-detailed breakdown is a hindrance rather than a facilitator. Unfortunately, as far as the breakdown levels are concerned, a generally applied rule of thumb can hardly be formulated.

It is wise to develop the activity structure by applying the top-down approach first. The desire to achieve completeness, however, dictates that in order to have the necessary control, the activity structure should be refined again. But this time the bottom-up approach should be used; one can start building the structure at the level of elementary activities and go through the bigger ones in order to get the project result as a whole.

Insofar as the first-line breakdown of the project activities encompasses the entire project cycle based on the activity structure and taking into consideration the structure of function vehicles, one can detail the cost and time constraints for the entire project. It completes the formation of all three primary targets of the project, not to mention the pertaining feasibility studies and the selection of the project option to be implemented, which is based on the feasibility studies.

The activity structure can be applied to such purposes as the following:

- analyzing the relationship between the activities in order to select the right form of depicting the project time plan and to prepare the plan itself (see Chapter 4)
- analyzing the workflow interdependence in order to formulate the project strategy (see Chapter 6)
- exploring the uncertainty factors of the implementation process and analyzing the risks that derive from them so that a risk policy can be developed (see Chapter 9)
- analyzing the uncertainty factors and the interdependence in order to make decisions on the organizational form used for project implementation (see Chapter 10)
- making decisions on the resource demand necessary for project implementation (see Chapter 4)
- rendering a basis for a monitoring and controlling system of the project implementation, including the necessary management information system, as well (see Chapter 8)
- determining the milestone events of project implementation (see Chapter 4).

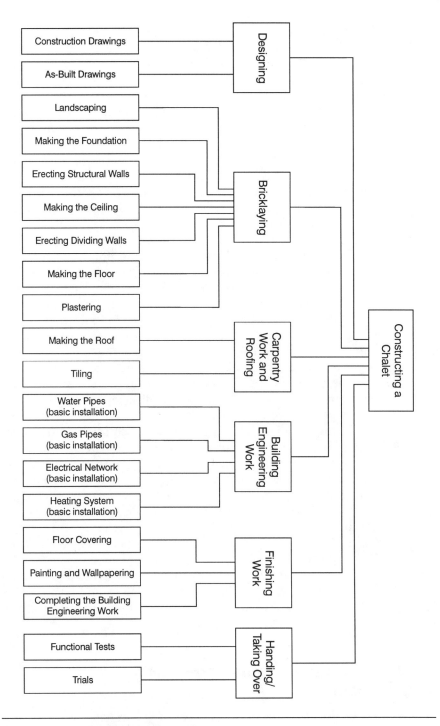

Figure 3.3   The Activity Structure

While creating the activity structure, the most generally applicable solution is a first-line breakdown of the project activities, which is based on the professional content of the activities. An activity structure expanded in this manner can be used in all of the different ways and with all of the different aims mentioned above. What also justifies the applicability of that kind of activity structure is that during the definition of time and cost constraints of the project, this approach can be used in any type of project.

All of these attributes apply only in a limited form to those activity structures where the first-line breakdown is the one applied in the function structure or that is used with the structure of the function vehicles. In both cases, one should say that only if the individual functions or function vehicles can be separated from each other, the activity structure formulated in this way can be handled and used with ease in the ways and with the aims listed earlier. In other words, the application of the previously mentioned breakdown considerations are suitable when the individual functions are independent from each other, regarding their operability or, at the worst, when they are interconnected only by low-complexity process interdependence. This phenomenon could be relevant to the structure of function vehicles when the different parts of the function vehicles operate similarly interconnected parts of the operating process.

The activity structure based on the geographical locations of the implementation is significant as an additional or complementary tool when the project implementation takes place at different locations. The breakdown resulting from the activity structure, developed from the points of view of the organizations participating in the implementation, can be interpreted similarly. It is also prepared as a complementary tool when more than one contributor takes part in the implementation (e.g., in a traditional contract), or when the client applies the linear-functional-organizational form during the project implementation. This is true even when it is used for managing the implementation activities—i.e., when different functional departments are involved in the project.

The need for the activity structure, based on the phases of the project cycle, arises when the activity analysis and review of the activities for the project in its entirety (e.g., in order to elaborate the cost and time constraints) become essential.

Implications of an Integrated Approach to Project Structures

The different kinds of project structure plans have been discussed separately so far, although it was inevitable to refer to interrelationships between them. It is more so inevitable since one could get to the activity structure that explores the implementation process through the structure of the function vehicles, which can be formulated based on the function structure. In this way, the different project structure plans are not independent of each other. At the same time, it was also hinted that the structure plans of a project considered jointly enrich the practice of project management by making the activity of managing project implementation strategic oriented. The need for strategic-oriented project management has been emphasized several times, especially when the project cycle was discussed. We have to understand, however, that the possibility, or rather the methodological basis for it, is ensured by the joint interpretation of the structure plans presented here. The approach that uses each one of the different structure plans, deliberately considering the need for strategy-oriented project management, and applies these plans jointly results in an integrated approach to project structure plans. However, the integrated structure plan does not necessarily infer a new structure plan. It implies that the different structure plans are investigated together, and, based on their joint analyses, new conclusions are available, enhancing not only the project implementation itself but also creating a cornerstone to help achieve strategic objectives through the use of projects.

This approach cannot be considered widespread these days. The activity structure plan is generally applied to any type of project. However, it could be detrimental in noncapital investment-engineering projects where, because of quantifiability problems, there is a greater need for developing the function and the function vehicles' structures and, as a corollary, concerning the integrated approach to structure plans. In capital investment-engineering projects, the situation is much better in this respect, especially if the process design and the accompanying list of equipment that are generally applied here, based on their essential characteristics, can be considered a kind of function and function vehicles' structures. We must add that their application in a way that would enhance utilization of strategic-oriented project management cannot be considered a generally appreciated method, apart from those projects that utilize process technology during the operation phase.

How does the integrated approach to structure plans of the project contribute to strategic-oriented project management, which serves the interests of the project client in the best way? What are the implications for those who are responsible for managing change by projects? Considering the individual structure plans, the purpose of preparation and applicability of a single structure plan was mentioned without emphasizing the integrated approach. Following is an overview of the possibilities that can be generally applied and are offered at the same time as the methodological means rendered by the integrated approach to structure plans:

- marking off the scope of the project result and the scopes of the project options, and determination of the time and cost constraints
- marking off different but interconnected projects within an organization, and dividing megaprojects into smaller subprojects
- elaborating the project profile, which is the starting point for making decisions on the project strategy.

Formatting the scope of a project result or that of different project options and determining their time and cost constraints can be considered decisive steps from the points of view of project implementation and practicality. The primary project targets are defined as the result of the above activity. These comprise nothing else but, on the one hand, the project result itself, which is directly connected with the achievement of the organization's strategic objectives. On the other hand, they imply the time and cost constraints of the project to be implemented, which are directly connected with the project result in this way. From among the primary project targets, in light of the interrelations mentioned earlier, the project result to be implemented has to be stressed. Its formation, at the same time, infers the marking off and definition of project scope. The primary project targets' significance beyond that lies in the fact that in this way not only the project can be distinguished from its environment, but also the expected project result can be determined more accurately.

This task can be carried out with relative ease in projects that are quantitative in every respect. The less quantifiable a project is, the more difficulties one may encounter. Thus, there is a need for methodological assistance. In this case, the integrated approach to project structure plans, which leads from the function structure through the structure of the function vehicles to the activity structure, is helpful. It creates a relatively accurate definition of those projects that are hardly quantifiable with regard to their content. As a corollary, more exact time and cost constraints can be detailed. After all, it is the integrated approach to the structure plans that is based on which strategic objectives can be transferred into projects in an adequate manner. In connection with this, it is worth mentioning that in certain projects, besides the basically positive content description, the negative or an excluding project-scope definition can also make sense. For example, in the case of a privatization project, competitors, representing a certain kind of *function vehicles*, could be excluded.

This question leads to the *end of the project*, which is connected to a great extent, beyond defining the scope of the project result, with the time constraints of the project. The question becomes significant when the project result cannot be quantified satisfactorily, and when it gets integrated into the operating functions of the organization step by step. In a quantifiable project result, even if it is integrated into the operating functions of the organization step by step, the achievement of the project result can be evaluated (e.g., by means of tests), which makes the end of the project determinable. Concerning projects that are different from the one mentioned above (e.g., transformation of the organizational structure), the project result cannot be directly tested. Yet, it is integrated into the operating functions of the organization step by step. In such a case, the phenomenon of completion also should have definite content and meaning, especially in external projects. Based on the integrated approach to the structure plans, the functions, the function vehicles that realize the functions, and the activities that realize the function vehicles can be specified more precisely in such a project. The milestone events, based on both the step-by-step implementation of the project and the step-by-step start-up of the project result, can be specified also by means of the integrated approach to the project structure plans.

For the sake of completeness, we should speak about the *beginning of the project*. The significance of the beginning is considerably smaller than the ending and cannot be defined exactly. Generally speaking from a theoretical point of view, it can be said that the transformation of strategic objectives or actions into projects can be considered as the first step of a project.

Owing to the diversity of the strategic objectives within the organization, in a given situation the number of projects undertaken can be more than one. In this case, from the point of view of their practicability, projects have to be marked off each other according to their content. If the projects are interrelated, marking them off becomes even more important. The integrated approach to the projects' structure plans provides a good basis for the professional who has experience in the given field to analyze the:

- relation between the operating functions, i.e., process interdependence of the individual project results to be implemented
- relation between the function vehicles of the projects, based on the process interdependence between the projects
- workflow interdependence between those activities that result in the creation of the function vehicles of the project.

These analyses reveal interdependence, or, to be more exact, they reveal the complexity of the interdependence that connects the individual projects. The complexity of the interdependence shows where it makes sense to draw the borderlines of the individual project scopes when the final decision is about to be made. In connection with this, the following general guidelines can be laid down.

1. It is wise to bring within the borders of the same project those function vehicles that are connected by complex process interdependence, or in other words, those function vehicles where the operability of the functions is made to work by different function vehicles mutually dependent on each other.

2. From the point of view of the workflow that brings about the function vehicles, those function vehicles that are interconnected by reciprocal workflow interdependence should be brought within the borders of the same project.

The pivotal role of interdependence shining through the rules mentioned above are, however, not deterministic. One should say instead that they form the basis for the decisions to be made in this respect. Practically speaking, the same rules give good guidance when megaprojects or superprojects are to be broken down into subprojects during implementation.

When project strategy is discussed in Chapter 6, project-strategy decision-making is based on the project profile. Then, the likely solution derived from the character value of the project profile has to match the character value of the client profile. Identifying the concrete character values in the project profile also brings to light a need for an integrated approach to the structure plans. Analyses made based on the integrated approach to the structure plans support the information demand necessary for elaboration of the project profile. In reference to interdependence and uncertainties described in Chapter 2 and encompassed in the project profile (see Chapter 6), it seems necessary to again stress that the interdependence and uncertainties, together with their characteristic values, can be explored in a given project, by experts concerned with the content of the project, based on the integrated approach to the structure plans.

Chapter Four

Planning the Project

THE SUCCESSFUL REALIZATION of a project will depend upon careful and continuous planning. The activities of all concerned in the project, including, where appropriate, external designers, manufacturers, suppliers, and contractors and all of their resources, must be organized and integrated to meet the primary target objectives.

The purposes of planning are to persuade people to perform tasks before they delay the operations of other groups of people and in such a sequence that the best use is made of available resources; and to provide a framework for decision-making in the event of change. Assumptions are invariably made as a plan is developed; these should be clearly stated so that everyone using the plan is aware of any limitations on its validity. Programs are essentially two-dimensional graphs and in many cases are used as the initial and sometimes the only planning technique.

This chapter reviews planning techniques for projects. The role of information technology is examined along with suggestions on the relationship between cost estimating and planning. (More specific advice about information technology is contained in Chapter 13. It is also important to read this chapter in conjunction with Chapter 8 on project control, as the planning and control cycles are key elements in the understanding of project management.)

Time Planning

A plan usually consists of a number of discrete items of work, commonly referred to as activities or tasks, which have to be completed often in association with constraints arising from the type of work, the location of the work, or the sequence or continuity of the work. Some things can be done simultaneously, while others have to follow in a predetermined chronological order. One of the first outcomes that the project manager requires from a plan is an assessment of the project duration, that is, the total time required to complete all of the work.

A plan should be simple so that the planner and other users easily understand it. Also, it is a straightforward process to update a simple plan without the demand for feedback of large amounts of project data. However, a plan should be flexible so that all alternative courses of action can be considered. There is no *standard* plan that can be produced. All of us could consider the same project, identify a plan consisting of different numbers of activities, and all would be equally valid. However, there are established planning techniques, which will be discussed in this chapter. It is difficult to enforce a plan that is conceived in isolation, and it is therefore essential to involve the people responsible for the constituent operations in the development of the plan. The plan must precipitate action and thus must be available in advance of the task.

The bar chart, also known as the Gantt chart, is a common tool used in project management. A hollow bar positioned along a time axis to demonstrate start, finish, and duration denotes each activity. The space inside the bars can be used for output or plant costs figures, and there is room beneath the bar to mark actual progress. However, while the bar chart is easy to understand, it is limited in the information that it communicates; its main weakness is that it does not consider the interrelationships among activities.

Plans that do consider these relationships are predominantly forms of network analysis techniques: precedence diagrams—sometimes called activity-on-node networks—and arrow diagrams—sometimes called activity-on-line networks. These methods form the basis for about 90 percent of all project management software; the precedence method is the most popular.

A network diagram is plotted, resembling a flowchart. The network must have identified start and finish activities, and all intermediary activities must have at least one successor activity and one predecessor activity. Complex relationships might require several logical linkages in a network model.

A time plan calculates what is known as the critical path. Starting at time-period zero, the earliest start and finish times are calculated for each activity. The start activity will have an early start of zero and an early finish of *zero + activity duration*. The early start of the following or succeeding activities will be the same as the early finish. This process is repeated until the finish activity is reached and the early finish time is calculated, constituting the minimum duration for the project. If, due to the complex connections in the network, an activity has two different early starts, then on this *forward pass* through the network, the higher numerical value is always taken. A *backward pass* is then commenced from the finish activity, calculating late finish and late start. It should arrive back at the start activity with a late start of zero. Although calculations can be undertaken manually, most are now assessed using software packages. On each calculation, a path or paths will exist through the network, joining activities of equal early and late start (or finish) times. These activities on the path are said to have *zero float*, meaning that with any delay or extension, the overall project time will not be achieved.

This provides the planning time for a project. However, it assumes that all resources required for the project will always be available at the levels required and that cost does not matter; neither is a realistic assumption.

The planner is often faced with a degree of uncertainty in the data used for planning. (Chapter 9 deals with project risk and uncertainty in detail.) Most planning techniques inevitably use single-point, deterministic values for duration and cost, although practically there may be a range of values for these parameters. There may be times when it is more appropriate to consider the uncertainties of the project.

Resource Allocation

Work, identified as an activity, needs resources, which are the productive aspects of the project and typically include the workforce, equipment (plant), subcontractors, vendors, and raw materials. Sequences of activities will have been linked on a critical-path time scale, and resources will be allocated to each activity to ensure that efficient use is made of expensive and/or scarce resources within the physical constraints affecting the project.

Once the allocation has been made, the next step is to consider the total demand for key resources. There is likely to be competition between activities for resources, and the demand may either exceed the planned availability or produce a fluctuating pattern of resource use. This is known as *project resource aggregation*.

If the demand exceeds supply, resource leveling, also known as resource smoothing, is adopted to utilize the project float. Float can be used to adjust the timing of activities so that the imposed resource limits and the earliest completion date are not exceeded. If the float available within the program is not sufficient to adjust the activities, the planner could consider the resources assigned to each activity and assess whether the usage can be changed, thus altering the individual activity durations. Clearly, the leveling of one resource will have an effect on the usage of others. Consequently, resource leveling is usually only applied to a few key resources. Again, while simple resource-allocation problems can be tackled manually, it is common practice to use commercial project management software for this purpose.

In some cases, it will still not be possible to satisfy both the restraints on resource availability and the previously calculated earliest-completion data by leveling, and the duration of the project is then extended. In other words, the project plan moves from being time constrained to being resource constrained. This process is conducted with software packages, making use of sets of heuristic rules to perform resource scheduling. Heuristics requires some base criteria, usually a set of predetermined priority rules, and some procedures to allocate resources.

A typical heuristic might be similar to the following example.

1. Allocate resources to the activity having the least float.

2. Allocate resources to the activity requiring the largest number of resource days.

3. Allocate resources to the activity using the largest number of resources.

4. Allocate resources to the activity that precedes the largest remaining resource-days requirement

5. If a tie, allocate to the activity with the lowest sequence number.

A scheduled sequence of activities for a project on a resource-constrained model is the output from a resource-scheduling exercise using a heuristic. Very few of the information-technology software packages allow access to the heuristic rules, although some of the most expensive packages permit limited editing of the rules. If this facility is to be used, it is worth *benchmarking* or validating the selected software against known historical projects to ensure that the heuristic criteria are in line with the user's strategic and primary project targets.

Most software packages also permit costs to be entered, and the resource scheduling can also be defined in terms of cost optimization. Integrated project-management software will allow the user to select which of these types of plans is required. (Selecting software packages is discussed in more detail in Chapter 13.)

Cost Estimation

There is a need to include costs in a similar manner to the way that activity time is incorporated into a plan. This is a part of planning often referred to as cost estimation.

In theory, the unknowns—that is, the risks associated with a project—can be shown to decrease as the project progresses until at the project completion, the final cost is known with certainty. As the project progresses from appraisal to sanction, so the accuracy of cost estimation is also likely to improve. Consequently, when dealing with risk-management software, there is often a high degree of uncertainty associated with cost information (as discussed in Chapter 9); by the time project plans are prepared, it is common to accept deterministic or single-point values of cost.

The ability to build up project costs using an operational-estimating approach is common to most critical-path-based planning packages. This approach is based on the concept of considering the constituent operations necessary to realize the project and then estimating workforce, plant and equipment, subcontractor, vendor, and materials costs together with the overheads.

Recent changes and developments in information technology have significantly influenced estimating activities. The trend seems to be moving away from using information technology for data capture, manipulation, and retrieval in massive databases and more toward using it in integrated project-management planning packages.

Expert systems are also attracting considerable interest as potential aids to decision-making. In an advisory role, they could provide the necessary assistance to produce the cheapest cost estimate by allowing automated decision-making to select resources to match different workloads. Computer-aided estimating is established to varying degrees in most of the larger construction companies. (The role of information technology in project management is reviewed in Chapter 13.)

Planning Method Selection

The increasing commercial pressure on project managers to achieve predetermined time and cost targets combined with the power of the desktop computer has led to a proliferation of project-management software packages. These programs vary widely in terms of their modeling flexibility and simulation options but are designed to serve the same purpose: to provide project managers with power to plan the time and cost out-turn for resource-constrained projects.

The project manager is concerned with the three primary targets: time, cost, and quality of the project result. As specifications and contractual procedures can largely control quality, the mathematical planning model is required to represent the interrelationship between the other two factors. Risk-management software should be used for project appraisal. At the project sanction or implementation stage, a program should then meet the following main needs:

- detailed network-modeling facilities
- detailed cost and resource-modeling facilities
- intelligent resource-scheduling options
- progress measurement
- a comprehensive customizable report module
- export/import options.

Chapter Five

Project Strategy—The Means

I N THE PREVIOUS CHAPTERS, reference was made to the term *project strategy* several times without providing a detailed explanation. Project strategy is the basic tool for allocating risks and responsibilities pertaining to the implementation phase of the project cycle. Thus, formulating project strategy is a decisive step from the point of view of the project client during the course of the awarding phase.

The responsibilities and risks to be allocated are identified in connection with the primary project targets (see Figure 1.1). Ultimately, these responsibilities and risks are associated with the expected project result as a whole (completeness, quality, operability, and so on) and the time and cost constraints of its implementation. As a result of formulating the project strategy during the awarding phase, a certain arrangement of risk and responsibility allocation comes into being. The primary project targets, especially the desired project result, set during the project formation phase will be implemented within the frame of this arrangement throughout project implementation. In a well-prepared project strategy—apart from the possible modifications occurring in connection with the defined project targets—the primary project targets will be achieved in practically the same manner as they were planned.

Different players may participate in different roles while project implementation takes place. To enhance formulating project strategy, the players can be divided into two categories:

- clients who initiate the project, i.e., the organization for whom the project result is desired in order to achieve the strategic objectives
- contributors who bring about the project result during the implementation phase for clients.

The responsibilities and risks in question are to be allocated between these two groups of players when formulating project strategy. That is why formulating an appropriate project strategy, especially in external projects, is of great importance. Nevertheless, project strategy in the latter sense could entail not only a lot of lessons, but also serve as a good basis for formulating project strategy in internal projects. This is so especially if the contributors are the cost or profit centers of the client organization. Responsibilities and risks are different by nature; therefore, project strategy as a tool allocates them by using different means.

One of these means involves the type of financial settlement between the client and the contributors. Based on the type of settlement, allocation of risks associated with implementation costs is carried out. Types of contract represent another means of project-strategy formulation. With their help, allocation of responsibilities and risks associated with quality, operability, and completeness of the expected project result, as well as those associated with the entire duration time of the implementation phase, can be accomplished. Types of financial settlement and types of contract together provide the means for project strategy.

It has to be noted that in accordance with the traditional approach to project management, one-dimensional project strategy is in the forefront. This approach does not make a definite distinction between types of contract and financial settlement; to be more exact, it can be said that in accordance with this approach, types of financial settlement are treated as different types of contract.

The reader will see, however, that distinguishing between the two means makes sense. Regarding the primary project targets and referring to the responsibilities and risks to be allocated, the function of the types of contract is quite different from that of the types of financial settlement. Hereafter in this book, in order to emphasize the necessity of the two-dimensional approach, the term *project strategy* will be used.

Several different solutions for types of contract and financial solution have evolved. In this chapter, we provide an overview of the different types. Light will be shed on their basic characteristics, as well as on their possible advantages and disadvantages, which are interpreted from the project client's point of view, since project strategy decision-making falls under the umbrella of the client's authority.

This overview will constitute the basis for making decisions on project implementation strategy (which will be discussed in the next chapter). It also forms the basis for appropriate application of different prequalification and tendering procedures, which also belong under project strategy, in the broader sense of the term, and are closely related to project strategy means.

Types of Financial Settlement

The allocation of risks associated with the costs of implementation is put into practice by means of different financial settlements. As a corollary, the different types of financial settlement are to be differentiated, based on whether a certain type of settlement allocates the majority of risk to the contributors or to the client. Accordingly, the following types of financial settlement are price based, cost based, and target based.

Price-Based Financial Settlement

The financial counter-value paid by the client for the works provided by the contributors is fixed in advance in a price-based settlement. In this way, the financial counter-value to be paid can be considered as price; thus, the majority of the risks associated with the cost of implementation are borne by the contributors. With regard to project scope and content, if no changes arise during implementation, the cost of implementation borne by the client remain unchanged—i.e., the client does not have to face any further risks as far as costs are concerned.

Fixing the financial counter-value of the implementation can be accomplished with a single amount. If this is done, the term *lump sum* is used. The financial counter-value can be interpreted in units, such as the expected project result or different services, activities, materials, and so on necessary for project implementation. In this case, the price-based financial settlement is made up of *unit prices.*

Without giving a detailed analysis of the price-based financial settlement, it is necessary to highlight the fact that the lump-sum settlement is rather inflexible when both inflation and modifications occur during implementation. The unit-price settlement, on the other hand, is a lot more flexible, especially when dealing with modifications. As far as inflation is concerned, introducing the price-escalation form can decrease the inflexibility of the lump-sum settlement. While using unit prices can relieve the lump-sum settlement's inflexibility with respect to modifications, they constitute the basis for calculating changes in the lump-sum price regarding modification during implementation.

The price-based financial settlement has the following possible advantages for the client. Irrespective of modifications that arise during implementation, the costs of implementation are known in advance. Taking into consideration only this aspect, the client is able to prepare a perfect cash-flow plan appropriate to the implementation phase. Risks associated with the implementation cost, also irrespective of modifications, do not have to be borne by the client— a definite advantage.

The price-based financial settlement has considerable disadvantages, as well. A front-loading payment mechanism could originate, especially in the case of (monthly) proportional payments. As a corollary, those activities that are carried out at the outset of the contributor' performance will be relatively overestimated, while those that are conducted at the end of the contributor's performance will be relatively underestimated. In this way, willy-nilly the client provides the contributors with interest-free financing.

Owing to the inflexibility regarding cost effects of the uncertainties, another disadvantage is that the price-based financial settlement evokes two different kinds of extreme attitudes when potential contributors specify their tenders. One of them takes place when unrealistically high-cost contingencies are calculated in the bid price, especially in long-term projects. The other extreme attitude— sometimes it is conscious, and tenderers embrace it in order to improve their competitive advantages—occurs when the reasonable cost contingencies are not counted. When unrealistically high-cost contingencies are calculated, it increases the average level of tender prices. If the reasonable cost contingencies are not counted, it may cause financing problems for contributors during implementation and consequently slow the pace of implementation.

Due to the inflexibility mentioned previously, especially in lump-sum prices, the settling of price/cost consequences of modifications during implementation becomes uncertain, representing yet another disadvantage of the price-based financial settlement. This can lead to a number of conflicts between the client and contributors, which can in turn create a hindrance during project implementation. Since price-based settlements, especially lump-sum prices, presume the exact definition of the expected project result and/or the activities to be done in advance, this circumstance would reduce the number and extent of possible overlapping among the activities.

Cost-Based Financial Settlement

The client reimburses direct costs incurred by contributors during implementation in this type of settlement. Beyond these costs, the client also pays a fee—i.e., a certain amount or percentage of the direct cost—set in advance to cover the contributors' overheads and profits. Obviously, the cost-based financial settlement allocates the majority of the risks associated with the cost of implementation to the client.

The cost-based financial settlement is absolutely flexible regarding cost effects when modifications occur during implementation, However, it tends to develop a cost increase, which, with respect to implementation, is not justifiable. In order to impede or at least decrease this propensity, some mechanisms have evolved in the practice, which are covered in project management literature.

Following is a summary of possible advantages for the client when using the cost-based financial settlement. Since it is absolutely flexible with regard to cost effects caused by different uncertainties, bigger modifications are possible during implementation, and there are no possibilities for hidden cost contingencies for the tenderers. Because of the settlement's flexibility, the application of the cost-based financial settlement creates a possibility for increasing the number and extent of overlaps among the activities, resulting in a shorter duration time for implementation.

As is usually the case, the cost-based financial settlement has serious disadvantages, as well. Contributors are inclined to increase direct costs for at least two reasons: partly because the risks associated with the costs are borne by the client instead of the contributors, and partly because the cost-plus-percentage-type settlement directly encourages contributors to increase costs. The technical basis for settling costs should be a clear, correct, and controllable system of cost registration, which also increases costs for both the client and contributors. Another disadvantage is that the client does not get an accurate budget for the implementation in advance. Consequently, a reliable cash-flow plan, which would enable optimal financing of the project implementation, cannot be developed either.

An advantage for the contributors, in comparison with the price-based financial settlement, is that the cost-based type of financial settlement compensates the cost effect of the changing purchasing value of money (due to either inflation or deflation) in a natural way.

Target-Based Financial Settlement

Both academics and professionals have criticized the previously mentioned financial settlements first because of their rather unbalanced risk-sharing nature. Then, criticism is aimed toward the inflexibility of the price-based settlement and the cost-increasing tendency of the cost-based settlement. These represent reasons why financial settlements encouraging contributors to realize better performance on the one hand and save costs on the other hand have evolved. These financial arrangements are jointly referred to as target-based financial settlement. Although the main motivating factor that called the target-based financial settlement into being is to achieve better performance in some form or another, the application of it in many respects results in a more balanced risk allocation than in either price-based or cost-based financial settlements. This phenomenon is related to the fact that the target-based financial settlement can be applied only in combination with one of the other two types of financial settlement, which is why they can be considered, and not without good reason, as the basic categories of financial settlements.

The target-based financial settlement can be approached in the simplest way from the point of view of the primary project targets. Application of target-based financial settlements could be aimed toward the:

- expected project result (i.e., it could be directed toward achieving better performance with respect to some parameters of the expected project result rather than the predefined values)
- duration time (i.e., it could be directed toward achieving shorter duration time than a predefined value)
- costs of project implementation (i.e., it could be directed toward achieving cost savings in comparison with a predefined value, not excluding the possibility of penalizing a possible cost overrun).

Since one of the basic conditions for applying target-based financial settlements is the quantitative specification of the target values, the quantifiability of the projects in question could restrict the introduction of a target-based financial settlement that relates to some unquantifiable parameters of the expected project result. The conditions of applicability of target-based settlements can be described in connection with the above-mentioned phenomenon; these conditions include defining the target values in accordance with the expected project result or the scope of work to be done, and the financial counter value pertaining to achieving target values set in advance. They also include defining how to reward better achievements and penalize the worst achievements, in terms of money.

Theoretically, it is possible that all three of the above-mentioned targets could appear in the same financial settlement at the same time, but the fact that the target-based settlement can be applied in combination with one of the basic types of financial settlement creates further limits for application. For instance, in a price-based financial settlement, the cost target cannot be interpreted; separation of the costs referring to the actual deadline and the target deadline is practically impossible in the cost-based financial settlement; and so on.

When the target-based financial settlement is directed toward achieving better performance with regard to some parameters of the expected project result rather than with predefined values, it is referred to as a *parameter-target financial settlement*. It implies that the client can expect some extra output, due to the better parameters of the project result, and that she is ready to share this extra in order to encourage the contributors to attain better performance. Figure 5.1 depicts the operating logic of the parameter-target financial settlement by utilizing a hotel refurbishment project carried out in Budapest.

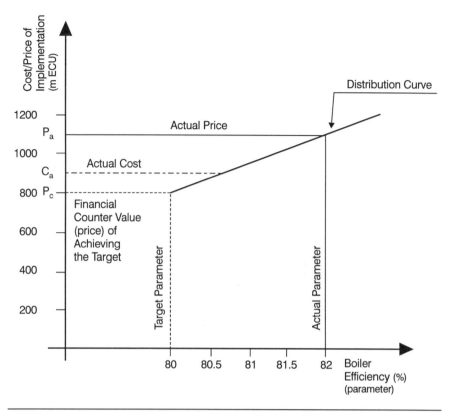

Figure 5.1   The Operating Logic of the Parameter-Target Financial Settlement

When the target-based financial settlement is directed toward achieving shorter duration time instead of a predefined deadline, it is referred to as a *deadline-target financial settlement*. It also implies that the client can expect some extra yield because of having the project result earlier, and she is ready to share this extra in order to encourage contributors to implement the project earlier. Figure 5.2 depicts the operating logic of the deadline-target financial settlement.

When the deadline-target financial settlement is considered, it should be noted that financial consequences of a possible late performance, in comparison with the target deadline, is not settled within the frame of this financial settlement but instead under the legal terms of penalty payments.

When the target-based settlement is directed toward achieving cost savings in comparison with a predefined value, it is referred to as a *cost-target financial settlement*. It implies too that the client is ready to

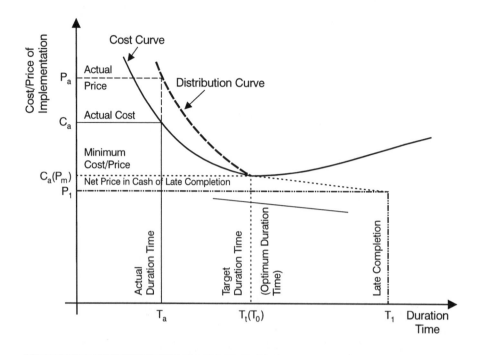

Figure 5.2   The Operating Logic of the Deadline-Target Financial Settlement

share the savings in order to encourage contributors to save costs. Yet it also implies that the client will share the cost overrun as well, to deter contributors from doing so. At the same time, it is also possible to define a guaranteed maximum price paid by the client and, accordingly, a minimum fee due to the contributor in question. Figure 5.3 depicts the operating logic of the cost-target financial settlement.

Upon reviewing types of financial settlement, it can be surmised that the two basic types, price-based and cost-based, bring about the allocation of cost risks associated with implementation of the project result in completely different ways. Although the primary function of the target-based financial settlement is to encourage better achievement, it also results in a less-unbalanced allocation of risks associated with the cost of implementation.

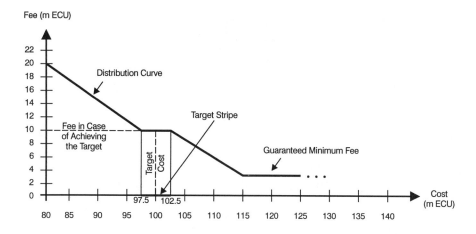

Figure 5.3   The Operating Logic of the Cost-Target Financial Settlement

Types of Contract

The means that realize allocation of responsibilities and risks associated with the desired project result as a whole and the entire duration time of implementation phase of the project cycle are the types of contract. Single contract types are differentiated, based on the natural characteristics of the contracts for allocating responsibilities and risks—i.e., whether a certain type of contract shifts the majority of responsibilities and risks onto the client or the contributors. In this way, types of contracts can be classified as traditional, turnkey, and management.

Traditional Contract

The point of the traditional contract lies in the fact that different work packages are formed out of the entire workflow of the implementation, and different contributors implement each of the work packages. The client concludes contracts for the packages with contributors who are independent of each other. In this way, each of the contributors takes responsibility and bears risks within the scope of activity at hand. Consequently, it is the project client who takes responsibility for and bears the risks associated with the project result as a whole (completeness, quality, operability) and the entire duration time of implementation. In exchange, so to say, for the greater responsibility and the greater number of risks, the project client can make modifications with more ease during implementation. Moreover, competition among the possible contributors can

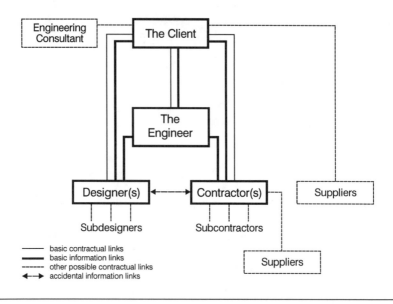

Figure 5.4   Relationships in a Traditional Contract

be broadened, and the client can exercise more direct influence and control over project implementation.

Figure 5.4 illustrates the typical relationships in a capital investment-engineering project that characterize the contractual arrangement in a traditional contract. This type of contract offers advantageous possibilities for a client. Among them are a relatively large-scale flexibility when demand for modification arises during implementation, large-scale influence on and almost complete control over the activities of implementation that bring about the project result, and, by forming work packages, broadened competition for the packages; consequently, general costs of implementation could be trimmed.

The traditional type of contract, however, implies some disadvantages for the client, as well. For example, it is the client who, willy-nilly, has to take and bear the majority of responsibilities and risks associated with the project result as a whole to be achieved (completeness, operability, quality, and so on) and the entire duration time of the implementation. Also, flow of information between the contributors is essentially one way pertaining to the entire workflow of implementation, and it is rather indirect since it is the client who mediates between the contributors. Another disadvantage is that the role of the engineer is decisive, while the scope of his responsibility does not go farther than his personal negligence.

The extent to which both the potential advantages and disadvantages could be manifested largely depends on the number of work packages in a given project.

Turnkey Contract

This type of contract utilizes a single contributor who takes responsibilities and bears risks associated with the expected project result as a whole and with the entire duration time of implementation. Thus, a client has only one direct contributor for implementing the project result. At the same time, possibilities for the client to exercise direct control and influence connected with the entire implementation workflow are lessened. By the end of the awarding phase, the client and the single contributor are contractually bound to implement a given project result—i.e., carrying out significant modifications—especially in a lump-sum price (see earlier section on price-based financial settlement in this chapter)—could result in long-running debates. In this arrangement, the single contributor has to take and bear responsibilities and risks in an individual and impartible manner. These obligations are not in contradiction with the employment of subcontractors by the turnkey contractor, since they have no direct relationship with the client. The considerably limited direct control and limited possibility to exercise influence over the implementation are balanced by an unambiguous taking of responsibility.

Several models of the turnkey contract have evolved. Apart from the semi-turnkey model—where the client is responsible for a certain part of the activities that are not directly decisive in regard to operation of the expected project result (as in the construction of an office block in a factory project)—these models can be differentiated by the role that the turnkey contractor plays in a given initial period of the project result operation. This role might involve, for example, training for the operators, maintaining the project result, transferring management methods, and so on.

The earlier-mentioned solutions mainly have spread in capital investment-engineering and information-technology projects.

Relying on the classic model of the turnkey contract, Figure 5.5 illustrates the general typical relationships that characterize the contractual arrangement.

The turnkey contract offers possible advantages for a client. For example, the client has a single direct contributor during the entire implementation phase. This contributor—the turnkey contractor—has an individual and impartible responsibility and bears the risks pertaining both to the implementation of the project result and the entire duration time of the implementation. Also, the size of the team managing the project—or rather the number of those who are

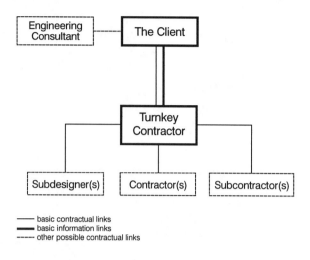

Figure 5.5   Relationships in the Turnkey Contract

involved in managing the project—can be cut down considerably, since a great part of the management services associated with the implementation phase is provided by the turnkey contractor. Owing to the individual responsibility and the same bearing of risks, the number and extent of overlapping between the activities can be increased. Consequently, the duration time of the implementation can be decreased—another advantage. Also, fast and direct flow of information is possible between the main participating organizations (i.e., the client and the turnkey contractor) involved in the implementation.

The turnkey contract also may pose disadvantages for the client. Because the client concludes a single contract with a single contributor until the end of the awarding phase, when demands for modification arise during implementation, her hands are tied a great deal. Also, when comparing the turnkey contract with the traditional type, one realizes that the client has only limited possibilities to influence and control the entire workflow, since the implementation process as a whole is concentrated in the hands of the turnkey contractor. Another disadvantage that may occur when applying a turnkey contract is that the competition is limited, as the number of possible contributors able to take responsibilities and bear risks is also limited.

Management Contract

What brought the management contract into being is the desire to preserve in one single type of contract the possibility for direct client control over implementation on the one hand, which is made possible by the traditional-type contract. On the other hand, it was desired to preserve the advantages of the individual and impartible responsibility offered by the turnkey contract. A number of models have been elaborated within this type of contract. Taking into consideration the characteristics of these models, the simpler ones are similar to traditional-type contracts, while the others come closer to the turnkey contract. Thus, the management-contract models create a kind of continuity between the traditional contract and the turnkey contract. It can be said in general, though, that the aim set in the course of elaborating this type of contract—i.e., unifying the advantages of the other two types of contracts—has been obtained only to a certain extent. The degree of obtaining this aim depends on the position that the management contractor, a special player who appeared in the scene along with the management contract, takes between the client and the contributors. This new contributor, the management contractor, takes over from the client a certain part of responsibilities and risks (which can be significant in a given model) associated with the project-implementation phase, while the advantages derived from forming different work packages are also obtainable. The management contractor establishes legal relations with the contributors on behalf of the client, and in this way supplements the client's inability to take responsibilities and bear risks. At the same time, the management contractor acts as a *client's agent.*

It should be noted that at present the management contract has been used mainly in big capital investment-engineering projects, such as airports. Yet essentially, solutions that are similar to some model of the management contract were used for implementing complex research and development projects, such as computer-based bank giro systems. The simple management, design and construction, and project management service models got rooted in the practice. Figure 5.6 illustrates the typical relationships that characterize the contractual arrangement in the design and construction model, frequently used in the management-type contract.

Highlights of the most essential advantages of the management contract for the client include the following. Since the different parts of the implementation phase are carried out by a number of contributors, based on forming work packages (similar to the traditional-type contract), the competition also could be broadened among the contributors. The client, by means of the management contractor, could enjoy a relatively large-scale flexibility when demands for modification

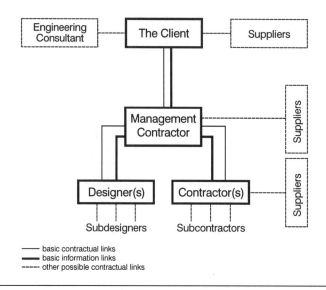

Figure 5.6   Relationships in the Design and Construction Model of the Management Contract

arise during the implementation. Also, the client, through the management contractor, has the possibility of influencing the workflow and exercising large-scale control over implementation. Owing to the coordination exercised by the management contractor, the number and size of overlapping between the activities can be increased. Thus, the entire implementation duration time can be shortened, as with the turnkey contract, representing yet another advantage for the client. Project management services with respect to implementation are provided by the management contractor for the client, which makes it possible to reduce the size of the team, the number of those who are involved in managing the project, which is also similar to the turnkey contract.

Along with the advantages, mainly in comparison with the characteristics of a turnkey contract, a couple of disadvantages also should be mentioned. The management contractor's obligation regarding responsibilities and risks associated with the project result and the entire implementation duration time is not literally as individual and impartible as in a turnkey contract. The flow of information between the contributors, here too, remains more or less indirect.

In the previous paragraphs, distinction between types of contract was made based on their characteristics for allocating responsibilities and risks regarding implementation, that is, whether it is the client or the contributors who have to take on more burden in this regard. Regarding formulation of project strategy, a further distinction, based on the integrative capacity of the different types of contract pertaining to the entire workflow of implementation, becomes necessary.

The turnkey contract, which is manifested in taking individual and impartible responsibility and bearing risks in the same manner, has a full-scale integrative capacity with regard to the client, since the pertaining allocation of risks and responsibilities could originate when the entire implementation phase belongs to a single contractor. Opposed to this, the integrative capacity of the traditional contract is limited to a great extent, as it presumes splitting up the entire implementation workflow. The more work packages that are formed or the more contributors are involved by the client, the less a traditional arrangement possesses integrative capacity. In this respect, the management-type contract is also an in-between category. The relative measure of its integrative capacity, from the point of view of the client, depends considerably on the position of the management contractor—i.e., it depends on his role playing between the client and the contributors, based on the characteristics of a given model.

Chapter Six

Project Strategy— Making Decisions

I N THE PREVIOUS CHAPTER, an overview of the means of project strategy was given; types of financial settlement and types of contract were introduced. We learned about different types of financial settlement and contract that may be applied in a number of combinations in different projects. Different combinations of financial settlement and contract types infer different ways and natures of responsibility and risk allocation among the participants of project implementation. Thus, it is the client's decision regarding which of the contract types and financial settlements will be used for the implementation phase, directly bringing about the desired project result. Making decisions such as this is one of the cornerstones of successful project implementation. The consequences of the decision are also decisive from the point of view of achieving strategic objectives in the client's organization by use of projects.

Nevertheless, making decisions on financial settlement and contract type in a given project is in essence making decisions on project strategy in a narrow sense. In a broad sense, project strategy means selecting a certain mode of tendering procedures and the occasionally implied prequalification procedures, as well. Both tendering and prequalification procedures are parts of project strategy in a broad sense, since the concrete application of these means is determined in many ways by the outcomes of making decisions on project strategy in a narrow sense.

Based on these considerations, this chapter introduces a structured and methodologically established decision-making approach to project strategy in a narrow sense. Beyond this, the chapter presents the effects and consequences of project strategy, in a narrow sense, exerted on the application of different types of tendering and the use of prequalification. For the sake of a better understanding of these interrelationships, a brief overview of types of tendering and prequalification will be given in this chapter also.

A Decision-Making Approach to Formulating Project Strategy

The method introduced here regarding project strategy decision-making intimates a structured and systematic procedure. It is indispensable, however, to further discussion to touch upon two important questions before introducing the tools for making decisions: What are the bases for making project strategy decisions? What is considered to be sound project strategy?

The second chapter introduced the inherent characteristics of the project-implementation process, namely uncertainty and interdependence, and the strong interrelations existing between them were also discussed. The previous chapter differentiated the types of contract, based on their integrative capacity too, with regard to the entire implementation phase. The previous chapter also showed that different types of financial settlement prompt different allocations of risks associated with the cost of implementation.

As a corollary, different characteristics of various projects, from the point of view of effective and proper project implementation, call for different allocation of responsibilities and risks between the client and contributors. At the same time, a project client should be aware of his own characteristics as well, since different types of contract imply different advantages and disadvantages for a client. In certain cases, these possible disadvantages (in some special cases, the possible advantages too) are expressly burdens for a project client. Thus, the question of whether a client, based on his organizational capabilities, is able to cope with certain disadvantages of a certain type of contract emerges. Simultaneously, it should be remembered that a client could follow goals associated with primary project targets during the course of project implementation that should be manifested in the arrangement of the financial settlement used for project implementation. Therefore, as a starting point for project strategy decisions when dealing with a given project and client, one should assure that both the contract and financial settlement (considering integrative capacity and risk and responsibility allocations) are in accordance with the dominant project characteristics, as well as with characteristics and goals relating to the client's primary project targets.

From the answer given to the first question asked earlier comes the reply to the second question. Obviously, both type of contract and type of financial settlement should interpret the phenomenon of sound project strategy.

The project strategy could be considered sound if the type of contract used for the implementation, with respect to its integrative capacity, is capable of integrating the dominant project interdependence to a single contributor. This requirement serves as a guideline when forming work packages for the entire implementation process (e.g., such as with a traditional contract) comes to the forefront. With regard to the forming of these packages, the following rules of thumb should be considered.

- All those work packages that are interconnected by reciprocal workflow interdependence should be placed with the same contributor.
- Marking off work packages alongside the borderline of sequential workflow interdependence is not wise if the separated activities result in creating function vehicles (parts of the expected project result) that are interconnected by complex process interdependence, owing to operating functions that are performed by the function vehicles in question.
- In order to utilize economy of scale (as one of the consequences of scale interdependency), it is also wise to be aware of the requirements of the first two rules.

The project strategy could be considered sound if the type of financial settlement chosen for implementation results in an allocation of risks, associated with the costs of implementation, that corresponds to the capabilities of the involved parties, regarding what they can handle and whether they can control the cost effects of risks. In other words, the participants of the project game should bear cost risks in a way that is in proportion to their influence relating to uncertainties.

Thus, detailing a sound project strategy, in the narrow sense of the word, involves analyzing interdependence, uncertainties, and clients' characteristics and goals relevant to the primary project targets.

The dominant interdependence characteristic to a given project works as a compass pointing to the type of contract, based on its integrative capacity, that allows a client to handle the project implementation phase. At the same time, the dominant uncertainties of a given project also indicate the type of financial settlement best for sound allocation of risks associated with the costs of implementation.

Project strategy decisions in a narrow sense can be made with more ease if both interdependence and uncertainties are depicted in a project profile. It is then possible to indicate the measure of presence as characteristic values of different uncertainties and interdependence.

A basic model of the project profile is illustrated in Figure 6.1, which shows, based on the extremes of the implied characteristic values, how a single characteristic exerts influence over decision-making on project strategy.

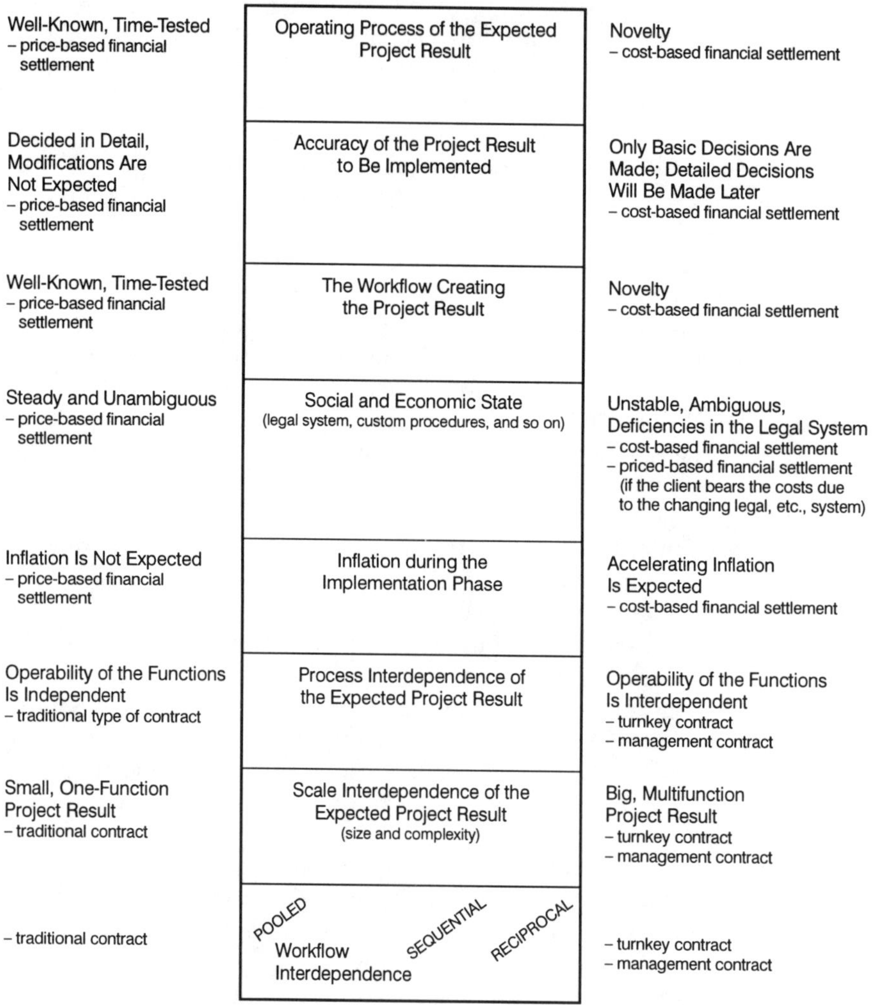

Well-Known, Time-Tested – price-based financial settlement	Operating Process of the Expected Project Result	Novelty – cost-based financial settlement
Decided in Detail, Modifications Are Not Expected – price-based financial settlement	Accuracy of the Project Result to Be Implemented	Only Basic Decisions Are Made; Detailed Decisions Will Be Made Later – cost-based financial settlement
Well-Known, Time-Tested – price-based financial settlement	The Workflow Creating the Project Result	Novelty – cost-based financial settlement
Steady and Unambiguous – price-based financial settlement	Social and Economic State (legal system, custom procedures, and so on)	Unstable, Ambiguous, Deficiencies in the Legal System – cost-based financial settlement – priced-based financial settlement (if the client bears the costs due to the changing legal, etc., system)
Inflation Is Not Expected – price-based financial settlement	Inflation during the Implementation Phase	Accelerating Inflation Is Expected – cost-based financial settlement
Operability of the Functions Is Independent – traditional type of contract	Process Interdependence of the Expected Project Result	Operability of the Functions Is Interdependent – turnkey contract – management contract
Small, One-Function Project Result – traditional contract	Scale Interdependence of the Expected Project Result (size and complexity)	Big, Multifunction Project Result – turnkey contract – management contract
– traditional contract	POOLED SEQUENTIAL RECIPROCAL Workflow Interdependence	– turnkey contract – management contract

Figure 6.1   Framework of the Project Profile

The project profile is a column-like setting encompassing the interdependence and uncertainties characteristic to a project. Each of the characteristics has a quadrant, and it is wise to divide them into three to five fields. It is then possible to mark one of the fields, thus clearly indicating the measure of presence or value of a particular characteristic. After marking each characteristic value and connecting them to each other, the project profile can be depicted (see Figure 6.3).

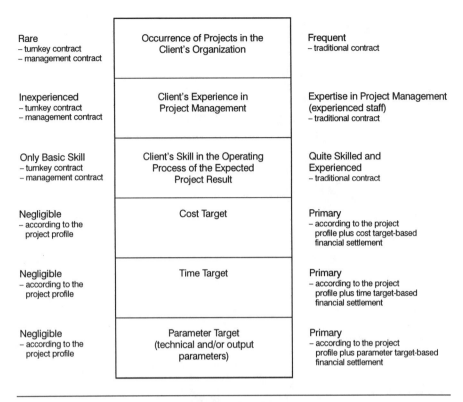

Rare – turnkey contract – management contract	Occurrence of Projects in the Client's Organization	Frequent – traditional contract
Inexperienced – turnkey contract – management contract	Client's Experience in Project Management	Expertise in Project Management (experienced staff) – traditional contract
Only Basic Skill – turnkey contract – management contract	Client's Skill in the Operating Process of the Expected Project Result	Quite Skilled and Experienced – traditional contract
Negligible – according to the project profile	Cost Target	Primary – according to the project profile plus cost target-based financial settlement
Negligible – according to the project profile	Time Target	Primary – according to the project profile plus time target-based financial settlement
Negligible – according to the project profile	Parameter Target (technical and/or output parameters)	Primary – according to the project profile plus parameter target-based financial settlement

Figure 6.2   Framework of the Client Profile

Making decisions based solely on the project profile should not be considered a definite answer. One should also assess whether the project strategy derived from the project profile is in compliance with the client's characteristics. For example, even though a certain arrangement of a traditional contract looks sound with regard to interdependence, the client's capabilities for dealing with the risks and responsibilities associated with the expected project result as a whole and the entire implementation duration time should also be evaluated. At the same time, it is necessary to evaluate whether there is a need for some type of target-based financial settlement. Both the client's characteristics and goals pertaining to the primary project targets can be depicted in a client profile (see Figure 6.2).

Based on the extremes of the implied characteristic values, Figure 6.2 shows the necessary modifications relating to project strategy, elaborated solely on the project profile. The client profile setting resembles the project profile setting. The characteristics are also in quadrangles, which should be divided into three to five fields. One

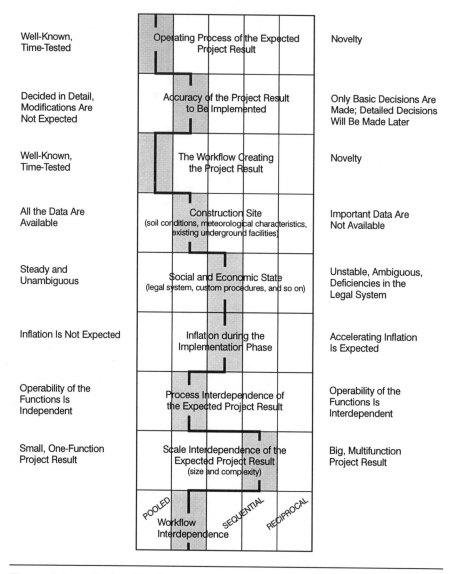

Well-Known, Time-Tested	Operating Process of the Expected Project Result	Novelty
Decided in Detail, Modifications Are Not Expected	Accuracy of the Project Result to Be Implemented	Only Basic Decisions Are Made; Detailed Decisions Will Be Made Later
Well-Known, Time-Tested	The Workflow Creating the Project Result	Novelty
All the Data Are Available	Construction Site (soil conditions, meteorological characteristics, existing underground facilities)	Important Data Are Not Available
Steady and Unambiguous	Social and Economic State (legal system, custom procedures, and so on)	Unstable, Ambiguous, Deficiencies in the Legal System
Inflation Is Not Expected	Inflation during the Implementation Phase	Accelerating Inflation Is Expected
Operability of the Functions Is Independent	Process Interdependence of the Expected Project Result	Operability of the Functions Is Interdependent
Small, One-Function Project Result	Scale Interdependence of the Expected Project Result (size and complexity)	Big, Multifunction Project Result
	POOLED Workflow Interdependence SEQUENTIAL RECIPROCAL	

Figure 6.3   Project Profile of the *Old Country* Project

of them should be marked for each characteristic in order to indicate as characteristic value the measure of presence of the characteristics. Connecting the marked field to each other, the client profile is completed (see Figure 6.4).

Essentially, the client profile can serve a kind of qualification of the client's organization. It is not only used to make an assessment

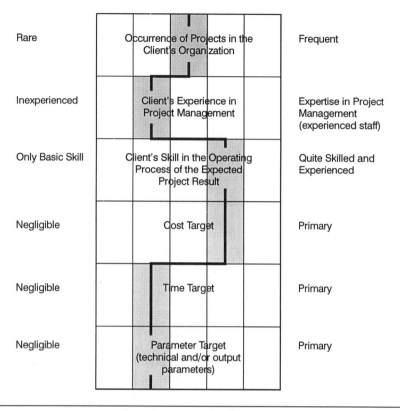

Rare	Occurrence of Projects in the Client's Organization	Frequent
Inexperienced	Client's Experience in Project Management	Expertise in Project Management (experienced staff)
Only Basic Skill	Client's Skill in the Operating Process of the Expected Project Result	Quite Skilled and Experienced
Negligible	Cost Target	Primary
Negligible	Time Target	Primary
Negligible	Parameter Target (technical and/or output parameters)	Primary

Figure 6.4   Client Profile of BÓRA Corporation

regarding the client's capabilities (in terms of knowledge and experience, organizational background, capacity, and so on) for coping with a certain combination of risks and responsibilities derived from an arrangement of a certain project strategy. The client profile is also used to bring to light the dominant goals associated with the primary project targets pursued by the client during implementation. The emerging goals could necessitate some target-based financial settlement in the course of developing project strategy. The order of importance of these goals could be dissimilar; thus, ranking them is essential in order to find the most suitable target-based arrangement to facilitate achieving the most desired goal.

The practical considerations and other implications of making decisions on project strategy, utilizing the above-described profiles, are explained by the following case study example.

A Case Study Example

The Client

BÓRA Corporation was established by four private individuals in 1990, and it was incorporated that year in Budapest; the founders have been the owners. Although the stock capital of the company has been raised three times, until the end of fiscal year 1995, the four founders have owned the shares in equal proportion.

After incorporating, the company started its business activity in the real-estate industry. During the first year of operation, it bought two medium-sized three-story buildings that were previously used for workers' hostels. The company not only refurbished the buildings but also fit them for office rooms. This idea proved to be a good one, and by letting the offices to other companies, BÓRA has enjoyed increasing profitability year by year.

During the third year of operation, the company launched a real-capital investment project: the implementation of a new building complex. It installed shops on the ground floor and office rooms on the other three floors. Since the shops and offices were rather luxurious, although they were small in terms of size, they attracted many small but highly profitable businesses interested in letting them. Running the buildings (involving heating, security services, and so on) was the responsibility of BÓRA Corporation. In general, it could be stated that BÓRA has enjoyed increasing turnover and increasing profitability.

The *Old Country* Project

At the end of 1994, the company incorporated a new business strategy and, keeping the acquired market segment, it decided to penetrate into the apartment segment of the property market. Because of the industry environment, especially the apartment segment (e.g., jockeying of big players), BÓRA aimed for a very special subsegment of the market: the Hungarian-origin population living abroad, who, once past the active part of life, plan to live the rest of their lives in the old country.

The Old Country Project was initiated in order to achieve the above-mentioned strategic objectives by building a complex in the countryside. The building complex itself would provide for its future tenants functions associated with living in the building (sleeping, eating, and so on), leisure time (library services, swimming, and so forth), and medical care geared toward senior citizens. Along with these basic functions, another group of functions will be provided, such as central air conditioning; security control; easy and safe flow of information among tenants and between tenants and operators; and such associated with running the building complex.

By the end of 1995, the company, with the help of different advisers and consultants, completed the project preparation, which resulted in setting the primary targets:

- the project result to be achieved (functions, capacities, qualities, layout of the building complex, and so forth)
- the implementation budget
- duration time of eighteen months for implementation.

Both project and client profiles and their actual characteristic values are shown in Figures 6.3 and 6.4.

Making Project Strategy Decisions

Considering the characteristic values in the project profile pertaining to uncertainties, one realizes that there are no significantly worrisome uncertainties. The most significant uncertainties are the social and economic states, especially the changing nature of the legal system, and the expected inflation rate during the implementation phase. Nevertheless, they are predictable; one can calculate the consequences in advance. All in all, based on the characteristic values of the different uncertainty factors, tenderers are in a position to make a reliable resource plan and cost estimation. Thus, they can estimate a reliable bid price, either in the form of a lump-sum price or in the form of different unit prices. As a corollary, the potential contributors are in a position to bear risks associated with the cost of implementation within the frame of a price-based financial settlement. Owing to the low characteristic values of the uncertainty factors, a lump-sum price looks applicable.

With regard to the characteristic values of the client's preferences in the client profile, it could be stated that the only outstanding goal is achieving cost savings in comparison with a target value. The question is whether the cost-target financial settlement can be applied in combination with the price-based financial settlement. Since the costs incurring in a contributor's organization are of no relevance to the client in a price-based financial settlement, the combined application of these two financial settlements is impossible. Now the decision-maker has to deal with a dilemma: change the price-based financial settlement into a cost-based financial settlement in order to pursue a possible cost saving, or abandon the cost target for the sake of the price-based financial settlement. Taking into consideration the characteristic values of the uncertainty factors, it is clear that there is no potential for cost saving, owing to the low characteristic values, while there is potential for a cost increase in a cost-based financial settlement. As a corollary, it seems wise to apply a price-based financial settlement and abandon the cost target.

When decision-making on the type of contract comes to the forefront, the characteristic values of interdependence in the project profile should be considered first. Both the process and workflow interdependencies are not complex; thus, a traditional-type contract looks sound, based on these characteristic values. Only the scale interdependence is considered complex because of dissimilar functions provided by the project result; it could even necessitate a turnkey contract. However, since the process interdependence is not complex—i.e., the operability of the different functions of the expected project result do not depend on each other—there is no real need for a turnkey contract.

Regarding the client's capabilities, it could be said that this client is not experienced in managing projects, although he has completed a couple of small projects. At the same time, the client is quite familiar with the operating process of the desired project result. Considering the above characteristic values with respect to the client's capability, we must conclude that he is not capable of coping with the responsibilities and risks derived from applying a traditional contract. If the client is going to hire an experienced project manager and divide the implementation phase into two parts only—construction drawings (design) and construction works (including start-up and tests)—the traditional-type contract could be considered. Otherwise, it would be wise to choose the management contract.

Further Elements in Project Strategy

Along with types of financial settlements and contracts, the project strategy in a broader sense involves the tendering procedure and prequalification. The tendering procedure, considering the implications of the project strategy in a narrow sense, refers to the competition among the actual contributors to be selected from among the bidders for the implementation phase. Types of tendering can be identified based on the relationships occurring between prequalification and the tendering procedure. In this way, the prequalification can serve as an evaluation of the possible contributors, based on certain criteria decided before the invitation to bid, in order to identify those who are capable of implementing the project result or a part of it.

Prequalification
Prequalification is the preliminary evaluation of the potential contributors, which has the ultimate aim of enabling the client to assess whether the applicants, based on predefined criteria, are capable of

participating in project implementation. Therefore, the criteria used for qualifying the applicants have to comply with the requirements of the project strategy in a narrow sense. Thus, only those applicants whose capabilities meet the risks and responsibilities derived from the chosen type of financial settlement and contract could be considered qualified.

It is self-evident then that the content and weight of a certain criterion are dissimilar in, say, a traditional type of contract and a turnkey type of contract. In a traditional contract, each contributor takes responsibility and bears risk within the limits of her own scope of activity, while taking the risks associated with costs is basically in accordance with the scope of activity. Contrary to the above, a turnkey contractor's individual and impartible obligations regarding responsibilities and risks pertaining to the entire implementation phase include:

- completeness of the expected project result
- quality and operability of the expected project result as a whole
- the entire duration time (or deadline) of the implementation, which includes start-up activities and tests, as well.

Of course, depending on the type of financial settlement used for implementation, the turnkey contractor has to bear cost risk to a different extent but in every case with respect to the entire implementation phase.

When a model of the management-type contract is applied, the extent of taking responsibility and bearing risk by the management contractor could vary between the two extremes staked out by the traditional and turnkey-contractual arrangement. The exact situation in this respect largely depends on the concrete contractual model in question.

These differences, regarding prequalification, which are due to different possible outcomes of making project strategy decisions in a narrow sense, are manifested in the first place not as a divergence from the basic structure of the questionnaire, but rather as differences involving the level of details and varying the weights of certain criteria during evaluation.

The prequalification process consists of preparing documentation, advertising, and evaluating applications. Since many time-tested standard prequalification forms are available, attention will be given only to evaluation, especially those aspects that are closely related to project strategy in a narrow sense, which will come to the forefront.

During prequalification, the applicant's capability is evaluated according to different groups of category. The scoring-point system is one of the most practical solutions for evaluating applicants, which could lead to a numerical ranking of the applications. In this way, the quantitative nature of evaluation can be increased—

i.e., using qualitative terms, such as *satisfactory* or *dissatisfactory*, can be eliminated. All in all, incommensurability can be avoided in this manner.

The relationship between project strategy and prequalification necessitates, to ensure objectivity, making in advance a clear decision regarding the scoring-point system. The decision should encompass certain considerations, such as the maximum number of total scoring points. Another consideration involves distribution of the total points between evaluation criteria. For example, defining both upper and lower limits in the form of scoring points in each criterion (instead of the lower limit, a nominal scale could be elaborated whereby the upper limit is gradually decreased) to enable ranking of the applications, based on a certain criterion. In this way, the relative weight of each criterion can be expressed. One should also define upper limits as minimum scoring points to be gained in each criterion on the one hand and pertaining to the total scoring points on the other hand. (For example, an applicant scoring less than 55 percent of the total points would not be accepted.) In this manner, unbalanced applications could be disqualified.

In light of the relationship between prequalification, project strategy, and requirements of the scoring-point system, it seems fairly obvious that, besides references and resources, construction and/or assembling experience are more important in an engineering project than experience in process design when, in the frame of a traditional contract, potential contractors are evaluated. Yet, it is extremely important in a turnkey contract to make sure that an applicant possesses all of the necessary props for being a reliable turnkey contractor. Taking into consideration the above example, a set of props would include:

- full-scale knowledge and experience relating to the operating process of the desired project result
- a reliable quality-assurance system enabling the turnkey contractor to control interrelated quality issues
- a flexible management structure so that a huge number of subcontributors' activities could be coordinated
- good expertise regarding the implementation process in order to supervise subcontributors; and so forth.

All in all, it could be said that the necessary capabilities of a possible turnkey contractor should be measured in terms of intangible forces rather than in terms of physical resources. Obviously, different project results postulate different concrete criteria relating to the assessment of a potential turnkey contractor's capability. Likewise, depending on the nature of the project, traditional contracts also require different criteria when potential contributors are assessed.

Not only does prequalification assist a client with selecting capable potential contributors, but also offers a couple of further advantages, such as the following.

■ Unqualified applicants can save the cost of bid preparation, which results in lower overhead cost and, as a corollary, lower future bid prices in the long run.

■ Evaluating only those bids that are submitted by qualified tenderers results in:

■ time and cost savings to the client
■ reduction of the potential of accepting a bid submitted by an incapable tenderer.

■ The client can measure the scale of interest or the potential supply, while the potential tenderers can gain information in advance about the future demand.

These obvious advantages could offset the disadvantages. For example, because of the time-consuming character of the prequalification, it increases the duration time of the entire awarding phase. Also, clients are required to review all applications, which also increases both cost and duration time of awarding. Nevertheless, prequalification should not be used for limiting competition to a predetermined number of potential tenderers; all of those applicants possessing the capability to perform the work in question should be considered qualified.

If too few applicants meet the requirements, it is unwise to lower the qualification criteria. Instead of this, further advertising and/or extension of the deadline for submission could be a favorable solution. Last but not least, redesigning the project strategy also should be considered in such a case.

Types of Tendering Procedure

Tendering, as part of the awarding phase, is a procedure of competition by which a client would select the contributors from among those potential contributors—the tenderers—who have been considered capable. The way in which the capabilities of the potential contributors are assessed at the same time renders the basis for differentiating types of tendering. In other words, types of tendering could be differentiated based on the relationships occurring during prequalification and tendering. In this manner, the following types of tendering procedure can be identified: open, selective, two-tier, and invitation.

In the course of open tendering, submitting of tender bids is not preceded by prequalification; thus, each potential contributor is considered capable of implementing the project works in question. As a consequence, all those who have bought the tender documentation have the right to submit their offers, and every tender bid should be evaluated. In open tendering, it is not unusual for the applicant of the best tender bid to be subject to postqualification, which is similar to prequalification when it comes to content and aim.

When selective tendering is applied, only potential contributors who are prequalified for the work in question are allowed to buy the tender documentation and submit a tender bid. Thus, to reiterate, bidding is preceded by separate prequalification procedures.

A couple of versions of the two-tier tendering procedure have evolved, such as the two-envelope, two-step, and two-stage systems. It is common for any two-tier tendering procedures to include two parts. The first part of this process, among other characteristics, fulfills the duty of prequalification in some way. Thus, prequalification, to a certain degree, is part of the process, but it is not organized in a separate manner.

In invitation tendering, a client invites a few, generally one to three, potential contributors to submit bids. Thus, bidding is not preceded by prequalification, as in open tendering; nevertheless, only those potential contributors who have been invited are allowed to submit bids.

For the sake of completeness, it has to be mentioned that the phenomenon of serial tendering is also frequently applied. In reality, serial tendering is a combination of one of the first three tendering procedures and invitation tendering. In this way, the first part (project) of a big program could be awarded by competition, while the following parts (projects) are negotiated with the winner of the initial part. This solution is frequently used in complex information-technology projects, which are implemented in a stage-by-stage manner.

Since the tendering procedure helps the clients selecting the actual contributors—depending on the project strategy, one or more contributors—at the same time, it provides competition among potential contributors. Tendering is based on a set of tender documents, which comprise all those general and special conditions on the basis of which a client wants the project result to be implemented.

The tendering procedure and the underlying tender documentation offer the following advantages for both clients and potential contributors.

- Since the desired project result or a certain package of the implementation work is recognizable by all tenderers in the same manner, the possibility for a clear competition is ensured.
- Based on the above, the submitted bids are comparable, and ranking them becomes available. Thus, objective bid evaluation is ensured.
- Owing to the possible clear competition and the potential for objectivity, the client has the possibility of selecting the best bid,

the one that offers the most economical project implementation in the long run.

Tendering could also involve possible disadvantages, including having to prepare, analyze, and evaluate a bulk of documentation, especially when bidding is not preceded by a separate prequalification procedure, such as the open tendering or two-envelope system. It also could increase the potential of selecting the cheapest price-tender bid as the best bid, especially in direct competitive bidding, such as open tendering, selective tendering, and two-tier tendering, when some price-based financial settlement is used.

When considering advantages or disadvantages, one should bear in mind that neither of them is manifested to the same extent in the different tendering procedures. Clients should be aware of the fact that in many cases an invitation tendering could not provide the above-mentioned advantages, since the conditions and solutions offered could be different with each different tenderer. This situation could occur when novelty R&D projects or novelty engineering projects are considered. It could result in a very complicated and misleading bid-evaluation process, since the submitted tender bids are not directly comparable.

Project Strategy in a Wider Sense

As has been emphasized, prequalification and the tendering procedure are interrelated; both of them should be in accordance with project strategy in a narrow sense. The criteria of capability as a whole and the relative weight of each criterion associated with the capability assessment are subject to the type of financial settlement and contract. As a corollary, selecting tendering type and consequently the content coherence of the prequalification should not be independent from project strategy in a narrow sense. Tendering and the associated prequalification have to be adjusted to those responsibilities and risks derived from the outcomes of project strategy decision-making that should be taken and borne by the contributors. This approach could ensure that capable potential contributors would be selected at the lowest possible cost. The necessity is justified not only by the need for the most economic implementation of the project result, but also by the proper achievement of the client's strategic objectives.

Therefore, choosing which of the tendering procedures is applied to implement a given project is not an insignificant decision, although the given project strategy in a narrow sense will influence not only selecting the type of tendering procedure but also the content of the tender documentation. Developing a sound project strategy relies on the characteristic values of the project, as well as on the project client. The same characteristics, through the medium of the above project strategy, practically direct the selection of the suitable tendering procedures.

In this respect, from among the factors influencing decision-making on project strategy, the project profile is more decisive than the client profile; from among the means of project strategy, the types of contract have primacy. This is explained by the fact that the type of contract is what defines the contributors' responsibility with respect to the desired project result; it is nearly evident in a project that does not show significant uncertainties and complex interdependence. In such a case, not only the expected project result but also all of the implementation conditions can be defined in advance. Thus, depending on the complexity of the project result and competition in the relevant market, both open tendering and selective tendering could be applied properly (see Figure 6.2). Otherwise, two-tier tendering (two steps or two stages) or invitation tendering is more sufficient, depending on the novelty of the project result.

Since both tendering and the associated prequalification have to be adjusted, the responsibilities and risks derived from making project strategy decisions and the proper use of tendering and prequalification can contribute to a considerable extent toward managing risks associated with primary project targets.

Chapter Seven

Projects by Business Concession

IN EUROPE, PRIVATE-SECTOR projects have always relied heavily upon the turnkey approach for process and industrial facilities-type projects. Projects have been and are still being constructed under turnkey contracts, including anything from a supply pipeline to a refinery complex or a hotel leisure resort to a fertilizer factory. These contracts usually require multidisciplinary involvement with short construction durations, and the contractor carrying responsibility for all aspects of the contract from conception through to commissioning and often into operating the plant and training permanent staff for the client while being paid normally on a fixed-price lump-sum basis. The money is either obtained from operating profits designated for reinvestment or from the owners' borrowings as debt finance.

Public finance has provided most of the major infrastructure projects procured in the United Kingdom and around the world in the last fifty years. Monies raised from taxation by governments have provided all or part of the finance required for projects such as motorways, bridges and tunnels, transport systems, hospitals, prisons, communication systems, leisure facilities, and water and power plants. In most cases, the contractors undertaking the project were engaged on price-based contracts and claimed monies on measured performance or milestone achievement. Occasionally, when faced with major unquantifiable risk, the public sector has utilized cost-based forms of payment for contracts; but these cases are rare.

The fact that no money is free, even to governments who also borrow from the private sector and bear the costs of collecting taxation monies, has resulted in private finance again being considered for a number of major projects normally procured with public funds. Around the turn of the century, the use of private finance was common for major engineering-infrastructure projects like the Trans-Siberian Railway and the Suez Canal. Both projects raised private finance through bond and share issues, and then charged users of the constructed facility a fee in order to generate revenue to cover construction and operation costs, risks, financing costs, and a margin of profit. After 1945, most governments realized that public finances could supply infrastructure of benefit to the state cheaper than private finance, and the popularity of this financing mechanism declined.

The use of private finance instead of public finance for a particular project is only justified if it provides a more cost-effective solution. The financial plan of a project will often have a greater impact on its success than the physical design or construction costs. Often, government support to lenders of project finance in the form of guarantees has been sufficient to ensure that projects have been completed that would not have been commercially viable without such support.

This chapter considers the current market for concession contracts. It also investigates the particular implications for the project manager working on this type of project.

The Corporate Structure of Concession Projects

When governments or their agencies place major projects into the private sector rather than into the traditional domain of the public sector by using a concession, they create a new set of relationships that differs from more conventional projects. Hence, the terminology differs too.

The *principal* is the organization responsible for granting a concession and normally is the ultimate owner of the facility after the expiry of the concession. Principals are often governments, government agencies, or regulated monopolies. In other chapters, the term *client* has been used. However, in a concession, the principal grants a concession usually with conditions or requirements and then plays no part in the remainder of the project, as the concessionaire, usually known as the promoter, takes on former client responsibilities.

The *promoter* is the organization—or, more often, organizations—granted the concession to *build, own, operate,* and *transfer* a facility, which is the reason that these projects are sometimes referred to as BOOT projects. Promoter organizations are often construction companies or operators in joint venture, incorporating constructors, contractors, operators, suppliers, vendors, bankers, business ventures, lenders, and shareholders. The promoter will then use contracts secondary to the concession to appoint parties and organizations to undertake the project and carry the risk; some of them may also be members of the promoter joint venture.

For the remainder of this chapter, the terms *principal* and *promoter* will be used with the outlined specific meanings. A principal awards a *concession* to a promoter. The contract between the principal and promoter is known as the *concession agreement*. It is the document that identifies and allocates risks associated with implementation, operation and maintenance, finance, and revenue packages between the parties and contains the terms of the concession relating to the facility.

In the late 1970s and early 1980s, some of the major international contracting companies in a number of countries began to explore the possibilities of promoting privately owned and operated infrastructure projects financed on a nonrecourse basis under a concession. The acronym BOT was introduced in the early 1980s by the Turkish Prime Minister Turgat Ozal to designate a *build, own,* and *transfer* or a *build, operate,* and *transfer* project; therefore, this term is often referred to as the Ozal Formula.

A concession or a build-own-operate-transfer project, may be defined as (Merna and Smith 1996):

> a project based on the granting of a concession by a Principal, usually a government, to a Promoter, sometimes known as the Concessionaire, who is responsible for the construction, financing, operation and maintenance of a facility over the period of the concession before finally transferring the facility, at no cost to the Principal, a fully operational facility. During the concession period the Promoter owns and operates the facility and collects revenues in order to repay the financing and investment costs, maintain and operate the facility and make a margin of profit.

Other common acronyms used to describe concessions include:
- FBOOT: finance, build, own, operate, transfer
- BOO: build, own, operate
- BOL: build, operate, lease
- DBOM: design, build, operate, maintain
- DBOT: design, build, operate, transfer
- BOD: build, operate, deliver
- BOOST: build, own, operate, subsidies, transfer
- BRT: build, rent, transfer
- BTO: build, transfer, operate.

Many of these terms are alternative names for BOT and BOOT projects, but some denote projects that differ from the above definition in one or more particular aspects, but which have broadly adopted the main functions of the concession. Concessions can also be regarded as vehicles for privatization insofar as they are replacing

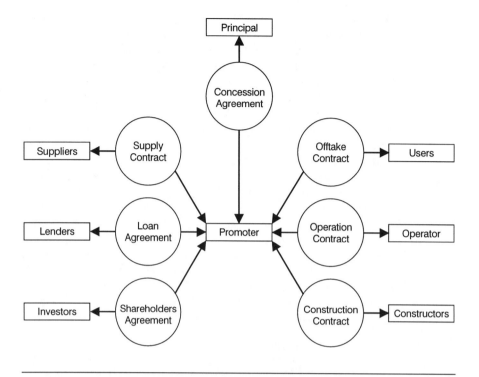

Figure 7.1   Typical Corporate Structure of a Concession

public-sector funding and no user charge with private finance and end-user charges.

It should be remembered that concessions in a pure sense involve total funding to be from the private sector, and the finance is guaranteed against the revenues of the project, that is, nonrecourse financing. Consequently, the promoter organization—although the concessionaire—usually has minimal capital assets and has to utilize secondary contracts to transfer risk to other parties. A typical concession structure is shown in Figure 7.1, and each of the secondary contracts illustrated are discussed below.

A *supply contract* is between the *supplier* and promoter. Suppliers are often state-owned agencies, private companies, or regulated monopolies supplying raw materials to the facility during the operation period.

In contract-led projects such as power generation plants, the user and promoter often enter into an off-take contract. Users are the organizations or individuals purchasing the off-take or using the facility itself. In market-led projects, however, such as toll roads or estuarine crossings where revenues are generated on the basis of directly payable tolls for the use of a facility, an off-take contract is not usually possible.

A *loan agreement* provides the basis of the contract between the *lender* and the promoter. Lenders are often commercial banks, niche banks, pension funds, or export-credit agencies that provide loans in the form of debt to finance a particular facility. In most cases, one lender will take the lead role for a lending consortium or a number of syndicated loans. In the event of default by the promoter, the leading lender usually has the right to operate the concession and hence earn the revenue to repay the debt owed.

An *operations contract* is between the *operator* and the promoter. Operators are often drawn from specialist-operation companies or companies created specifically for the operation and maintenance of one particular facility.

A *shareholder agreement* is a contract between *investors* and the promoter. Investors purchase equity or provide goods in kind and form part of the corporate structure. They may include suppliers, vendors, constructors and operators, and major financial institutions, as well as private individual shareholders. Investors provide equity to finance the facility, the amount often being determined by the debt/equity ratio required by lenders or the concession agreement.

A *construction contract* is a contract between the *constructor* and the promoter. Constructors are often drawn from individual construction companies or a joint venture of specialist construction companies. Constructors can sometimes take and have taken the role of promoters for a number of BOOT projects both in the United Kingdom and overseas.

Initiating a concession requires the principal to be committed to this vehicle and to support it throughout the concession period. After an initial feasibility study, there would normally be a prequalification stage as a basis for identifying suitable promoter organizations wishing to bid for a particular project. The principal prepares a concession agreement, based on the terms of the concession and the four packages. A number of suitable promoter organizations are then selected. The concession agreement forms the basis of the principal's *invitation to tender*.

The second phase requires a number of promoter organizations to assess the commercial viability of the project based on the principal's requirements identified in the concession agreement. A detailed appraisal indicates whether the project is commercially viable and whether the promoter should proceed with the bid. Secondary contracts are then identified, and their influence on the project is considered. If the promoter deems the project commercially viable, based on the secondary contracts, then a detailed bid is prepared on the basis of package documentation.

In the final phase, the principal initially appraises the conformity of each bid based on the contract documents, and then evaluates each bid according to the package weighting identified by the principal at the invitation stage. The concession would be awarded to the complying bid with the highest cumulative package score.

Debt and Equity

In simple terms, the financing of a concession consists of debt finance and equity finance. Debt finance is long term, usually accounts for the majority of the finance required, and is arranged at commercial rates through the lending contract. The equity is everything subordinate; it is invested first and repaid last. Members of the promoter joint venture usually supply it, although on major projects, secondary contractors or possibly institutional or private shareholders might contribute equity capital.

The contract between the promoter and lender to provide the debt finance can only be determined when the lender has sufficient information to assess the viability of a project. In concessions, the lender will look to the project in terms of revenue generation as a source of repayment rather than the assets of the project, or of the promoter group parent companies. The key parameters to be considered by lenders include:

- total size of the project—the size of the project determining the amount of money required and the effort needed to raise the capital, internal rate of return on the project, and equity
- breakeven dates—critical dates when equity investors see a return on their investments
- milestones—significant dates related to the financing of the project
- loan summary—the true cost of each loan, the amount drawn, and the year in which draw-downs reach their maximum.

A properly structured financial loan package should achieve the following basic objectives:

- maximize long-term debt—allow the project entity itself to incur the debt, which would not affect the sponsor's parent company balance sheet
- maximize fixed-rate financing—the utilization of long-term export-credit facilities or subordinated loans with low interest rates over long terms will reduce project risks
- minimize refinancing risk—cost overruns present additional problems to a project; therefore, standby credit facilities from lenders and additional capital from promoters should be made available.

One of the more recent developments in project financing has been the willingness of some promoters to consider ways of raising money other than purely relying on debt finance from banks. The interest in using bonds or shares, the so-called mezzanine financing, is growing. This may become much more common in project debt financing over the next few years.

Equity finance is usually an injection of risk capital into a company or venture. Providers of equity are compensated with dividends from profits if a company or venture is successful but with no return should the venture be loss making. Debt service in the majority of cases takes first call on profits whether or not profits have been generated; dividends are paid after debt claims have been met. In the event of a company or venture becoming insolvent, equity investors rank last in the order of repayment and may lose their investments.

The amount of equity provided is considered as the balance of the loan required to finance the project. The total finance package is often described in terms of the debt/equity ratio. In projects considered to have a large degree of risk, then a larger proportion of equity is normally provided.

The advantages of an equity investment are that equity may be used as a balancing item to accommodate fixed repayments, and equity investors are often committed to the success of a project, being organizations involved in the realization of the project. Providers of equity fall into two categories: those with an interest in the project (contractors, vendors, and operators), and pure equity investors (shareholders).

Public-Private Partnerships

As the identification of risks associated with any project develops in the early stage of project appraisal, it will soon become apparent whether the project is viable in terms of the investment required. Private project lenders and investors will only be attracted to projects that provide commercial returns on the capital invested.

Risks are conventionally measured in financial terms, as it is the most easily understood metric. However, risks are related both to the commercial project and to the risk of the project financing itself. Financial risks are associated with the mechanics of raising, the delivery of finance, and the availability of adequate working capital. Financial risks may include foreign exchange risks, off-take agreements, take, or pay terms; the effect of escalation and debt-service risk may arise during the operation phase when machinery

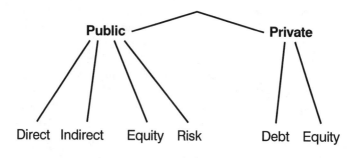

Figure 7.2   Spectrum of Public and Private Finance

is running to specification, but does not generate sufficient revenue to cover operating costs and debt service.

Considering Figure 7.2, if a project is viable, it could be financed solely from equity and debt finance from the private sector, as shown in the right-hand side of the diagram. Viable means that the identified risks appear commensurate with the investment to be made and the potential of realizing an economic return. If the project is assessed as too risky, it may require action from the public sector to mitigate the effects of risk for which the private sector would be liable. There are a number of measures that can be taken as shown on the left-hand side of the diagram. They range from sharing of risk, a relatively easy option, to the injection of direct finance, usually the last resort.

The public sector may provide equity in the form of land or, quite often, in the form of an existing facility with an existing revenue-generation stream, which is transferred to the promoter to provide additional equity funding.

A further stage would be the use of indirect mechanisms, including tax *holidays*, soft loans, periods of *grace* before loans would have to be repaid, and so on. These have an element of lost-opportunity cost; that is, the public could have earned more money by making a commercial loan to another customer but would have no capital-cost implications. Direct or capital-cost support would be used only if no other way could be found to make a much-needed project viable.

In a number of concession contracts, an existing facility is included as part of the concession offered. The operation of an existing facility often guarantees the promoter an immediate income, which may reduce loans and repay lenders and investors early on in the project cycle. In the case of the Sydney Harbour

Tunnel, Australia, project revenues generated by the existing bridge crossing are shared between the principal and the promoter, which enables the promoter to generate income to service part of the debt prior to completion of the tunnel. The concession to operate existing tunnels as part of the United Kingdom Dartford Bridge Crossing concession offered an existing cash flow but required the promoter to accept the existing debt on those tunnels. An existing concession also formed part of the concession agreement for the Thailand Bangkok Expressway; this arrangement required the operation and maintenance of an existing toll highway with generated revenues being shared between the principal and the promoter.

All of these examples indicate a need for a relationship between public and private sectors to finance socially desirable projects, which may not be the projects with the highest commercial viability or most robust revenue streams. Increasingly, attention is being given to collaboration as a method of expanding the provision of facilities to the mutual advantage of both public and private sectors.

Implications for Project Managers

Nonrecourse credits are not guaranteed by promoters or by host governments, and in the event of difficulties, financiers will have no recourse to promoters, assets, or governmental guarantees. The project stands for itself against lenders who only have recourse to the project assets and credits. Consequently, for the project manager, the task is more concerned with the risks of investment appraisal rather than with traditional technology-driven changes.

The project manager must appreciate the need for and the role of equity finance. In the United Kingdom, it is necessary to have a minimum of £50k to establish a public-liability company. The riskier the project, the greater the proportion required by the lenders in equity, as it reflects the level of commitment made to the long term of the project. Different levels of equity that different promoters offer to put on the project can result in the winning, or not, of a tender.

Projects with a strong business case capable of generating considerable returns will easily find attractive sources of finance. A project manager must recognize the significance of project financing and the new multidisciplinary opportunities provided for projects. This does not mean that project managers should be accountants or bankers but that the investment and revenue-generation issues must be studied, managed, and taken into account when making the overall decisions for any project that shows viability.

Utilizing private finance to fund a public project does not necessarily mean that governments have no role in funding arrangements. There is a genuine need for the project manager to be able to manage public/private partnerships. The project manager should be able to communicate well with both public- and private-sector organizations and be aware of their fundamental differences, limitations, strengths, and constraints in order to facilitate effective joint financial support for the project. Inherent in this type of work is the fact that the responsibilities are much broader based than in traditional projects, and the component of risk is much more significant. Decision-making under conditions of risk and uncertainty has always been a part of project management, but is especially important on a concession.

In the United Kingdom (UK), many concessions are part of the much-modified Private Finance Initiative supported by the UK government over the last ten years. Given the extent of support, it is disappointing to note the relatively low level of take-up on projects. There are many reasons, most of which have been addressed to some extent over the years, why the uptake is not developing. One of the factors was a shortage of project managers with the financial and project management skills appropriate for working closely with government. Other reasons included the cultural barriers, which needed to be overcome in order to cope with nontraditional operations and payment systems.

One of the UK projects that was initiated was the Birmingham Northern Relief Road. A concession agreement was signed in 1993, and yet the project manager has been so busy with inquiries and procedures that in 1998 work has still not commenced on-site. The 1997 review instigated in the UK by the newly elected government has now permitted a broadening of the use of private finance, in particular in the health and hospitals program and in leisure and education. However, due to the long-term financial commitment to projects, the current market would appear to be self-limiting. Once organizations had participated in a number of projects, the potential exposure to bonds or surety over a long period would seriously reduce their capacity to finance any new equity need. The UK government has also decided that shadow-toll roads, which place a commitment on the Exchequer for future years, should not expand beyond the current schemes. These limitations are serious but are unlikely to significantly reduce the increased use of concessions around the world.

Equally, as environmental pressures grow, a project manager on a concession would be involved to a much greater extent with protesters, environmental interest groups, and local community leaders. The part-traditional-client and part-traditional-contractor role of a promoter's project manager places greater demands on the project manager's skills, and in these situations adopts a role known as the *project champion*. As project champion, the project manager is the living personification of the project. As such, the functions are concerned with greater external acceptance and external problem solving because without them, there would be no actual project to continue to manage.

Chapter Eight

Project Control

PROJECT MANAGEMENT IS concerned with the setting and achievement of realistic primary targets for the project. This will demand effort—it will not happen as a matter of course—and it will require the dedication and motivation of people. The provision and training of an adequate project management team is therefore an essential prerequisite for a successful job, for it is the members' drives, judgment, and their abilities to persuade and lead that will ensure that the project objectives are achieved.

Managers of projects frequently encounter a mixture of technical, environmental, logistical, and physical problems. The style of management required for such work will therefore differ in many ways from that required in the relatively static surroundings of traditional-line management. The temporary nature of the project organization and the considerably greater element of uncertainty associated with most major projects could be particularly significant.

Uncertainty, as discussed in the following chapter, is the source of many problems encountered in project work and will influence appraisal, project implementation, estimating, planning, and contract strategy for the project. Excessive uncertainty can lead to continuous or multiple changes to the project primary targets, which usually reduces productivity and results in extra cost to both client and contractor. All parties involved in a project would therefore benefit greatly from the control of uncertainty prior to financial commitment.

The Role and Function of Control in Project Management

Control is concerned with regulation of the future. This implies the ability to predict or forecast the consequences of specific courses of action and necessitates decision-making under conditions of uncertainty. That is to say that the project manager must choose a specific

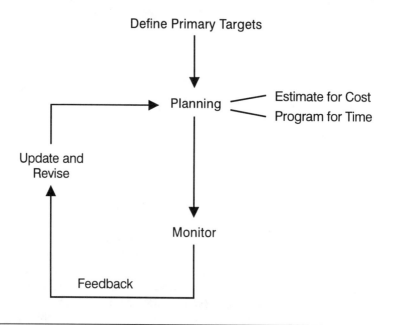

Figure 8.1   Planning and Control Cycle

course of action from those available, even though the consequences of the possible courses of action will depend on events that cannot be predicted with certainty. Control is an active process requiring timely decisions and implying drive and direction.

As has been stated previously in this book, the project manager must ensure that the project primary targets are both realistic and clearly defined. Both client and contractor are primarily concerned with their investments and the reduction of risk and uncertainty, hence, an increase in the likelihood of realizing the primary targets. When considering planning techniques, procurement, and other aspects of project management, there may be a tendency for each system to be thought of as a separate entity. Instead, the process of project management is integrative, and one important internal component is the planning and control cycle.

Control is exercised by planning and replanning the efficient use of resources, including money. If, during the implementation of the project, only the planned resources are utilized, then the predicted cost will not be exceeded.

As demonstrated in Figure 8.1, planning can only commence once the primary targets have been established. As demonstrated in Chapter 4, it is not possible to plan unless it is clear what the purpose of the plan is to be. Monitoring, sometimes referred to as control, is the process of comparing actual project progress with the plan.

Differences between the actual project and the plan do not necessarily mean that the plan is bad or that work has been wasteful. The original estimate may have been too optimistic so that despite a difference with the plan, work in progress is being managed well. Equally, it is possible that a pessimistic estimate had been made and, despite appearing to be ahead of the plan, progress is poor and is not being well managed.

Control is exercised within all parties to the project, as well as for the project in its entirety. The client has control of the scope of the investment to be made and has control over the commitment made at the sanction or implementation phase. The definition of the primary targets will have identified appropriate payment mechanisms and incentives within the chosen contract strategy for the project. The client can also contribute by minimizing the number of variations and changes during the implementation stage.

Contractors can also exercise control. The first opportunity is often through the commitments made in the returned tender bids, including the efficient use of resources to execute the project and by giving attention to sensitive elements of project cash flow. It is true for both parties that the scope for control diminishes as the project proceeds.

Tools for Project Control

One of the most popular project control tools is earned value analysis, a method that makes use of project "S" curves to compare expenditure and budget over time. Due to the use of the S-curve, the analysis is relatively easy to understand, enhancing the ability to communicate its findings to other project personnel. The main concept of earned value analysis is that it compares the value of work done with the value of work that should have been done.

S-curves examine the progress of the project and forecast expenditure usually in terms of money. This is compared with the actual expenditure as the project progresses, or the value of work done. All projects, whatever their size, are plotted against the same parameters, and characteristic curves can be more readily seen. The form of the S-curve is determined by the start date, the end date, and the manner in which the value of work done is assessed. Once a consistent approach has been established and the historical data analyzed, there are three significant variables that need analyzing: time, money, and the shape of the S-curve (known as the route). Since the

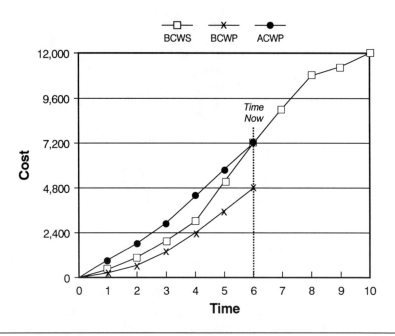

Figure 8.2   Typical "S" Curve of Budget Against Actual Cost Used for Control

expectation is that the route is fixed, then only two variables are left. The route is as much a target as the final cost.

The assessment and precise recording of value of work done is crucial to project cost control. This is described by accountants as *work in progress*; for example, project man-hours are usually measured weekly. The hours that have been booked can be evaluated at an average rate per man-hour, a rate representing the actual costs in the project. Materials are delivered against a firm order, so normally an order value and date are available. The establishment of realistic targets is very important if the analysis is to be meaningful.

Figure 8.2 illustrates a typical S-curve plot comparing budget and actual costs.

Budgeted cost of work scheduled (BCWS) is the value of work that should have been done at a given point in time. This examines the work planned to have been accomplished and the budget for each task, indicating the portion of the budget planned to have been used.

Budgeted cost of work performed (BCWP) is the value of the work done at a point in time. This takes the work that has been done and the budget for each task, indicating what portion of the budget ought to have been used to achieve it.

Actual cost of work performed (ACWP) is the actual cost of the work done.

Productivity factor is the ratio of the estimated man-hours to the actual man-hours.

Schedule variance is the value of the work done minus the value of the work that should have been done (BCWP - BCWS). A negative number implies that work is behind schedule.

Cost variance is the budgeted cost of the work done to date minus the actual cost of the work done to date (BCWP - ACWP). A negative number implies a current budget overrun.

Variance at completion is the budget (baseline) at completion minus the estimate at completion. A negative value implies that the project is over budget.

Schedule performance index is (BCWP/BCWS) x 100. Values under one hundred indicate that the project is over budget or behind schedule.

Cost performance index is (BCWP/ACWP) x 100. Values under one hundred indicate that the project is over budget.

Figure 8.2 indicates the ease with which complex information can be presented. At the project level, the project manager will be able to ascertain very quickly any significant underachievement and take the necessary action to correct the trend. The process could be repeated for individual work packages or combinations of packages on large or complex projects.

Companies in the oil and gas industries have developed a series of standard S-curves so that the performance of existing projects can be monitored. These curves have been derived empirically, and, when projects within certain categories do not follow the norm, investigations ensue to identify the source of the discrepancy. These curves have been put to a number of uses, including monitoring, reporting, and payment. They are not always used in the pure form; that is, further curves, such as productivity factors, can be developed so that certain aspects of the project can form the focus of attention.

Implications for Project Managers

The role of management is to exercise overall control of the project or contract from its inception through to the completion of commissioning. The primary function of the project manager is to define the primary targets of the project and thereafter to provide decisions, approvals, and guidance.

The project manager will need to delegate. To have confidence in the members of the project team, managers should be involved in their selection and in setting staff targets. The roles, constraints, and directions must be clear, concise, and understood by everyone with responsibility. As a general rule of thumb, it is suggested that control should be delegated as close to the work-face as possible.

The client will have identified the strategic goals for which the project is necessary, and these may be commercial, reflect the perceived needs of society, and/or have political overtones. The primary project-management targets identified by the project manager must be compatible with the strategic goals and should be clearly formulated early in the definition stage of project development. The dominant considerations must be fitness for purpose of the completed project and safety during both the implementation and operational phases. Thereafter, cost, time, and functional performance form the primary targets for the project. The potential for conflict between these objectives, as problems arise during project implementation, is obvious.

In attempting control, tolerances must also be specified—as range of acceptable variation in performance, float in the program, and tolerance and contingency allowances in the estimate. The greater the perceived uncertainty, the more flexible these criteria must be. Thereafter, the monitoring and performance against the plan based on the primary targets will determine the need for replacing, revision of estimates, and changes in project scope and specifications.

Quality assurance systems can assist the project manager in the setting and achievement of project primary targets and exercising control. Quality assurance (QA) is a systematic way of ensuring that project activities happen the way that they are planned. It is a management discipline concerned with anticipating problems and with creating the attitudes and controls to prevent problems arising. Through the QA policy and system and procedures, evidence is systematically collected and collated to demonstrate that all reasonable actions have been taken to achieve the required quality and identifying changes and variations involved in any project.

Quality assurance (QA) is usually associated with manufactured products and with complex multidisciplinary projects where safety and quality of plant operation are the major concerns, but in practice QA can be applied to all types of projects. The application of such systems to any project should depend on whether there is benefit. Care must be taken to ensure that the adoption of a QA system does not result in rigid adherence to unnecessarily demanding specifications. Neither must the system inhibit the flexibility and judgment required for the management of the uncertainties associated with the one-off job.

Misunderstandings and mistakes are prevalent in the early stages of development of multidisciplinary projects if objectives are not clearly defined and effective liaison between the various contributors is lacking. This can be particularly serious in the conceptual design, which should be rigorously reviewed to ensure compliance with the client's objectives. Regular audit of the project by a person or organization external to the project team is found to stimulate economy and minimize errors.

Chapter Nine

Project Risk Management

ALTHOUGH USUALLY PERCEIVED in different ways by different parties, risk is present to some extent in all projects. In some cases, the risk will be very low, and project management can operate with an assumption of the certainty of project data; in other cases, major unquantifiable risk will be the major consideration that could result in abandonment of the project. This chapter considers the nature of risk management and, given the increasing demands for effective project management to commence in the earliest possible project phases, provides insight into decision-making under conditions of uncertainty.

The chapter emphasizes the management of project risk, the philosophy, and methodologies. The mathematics that underpins each of the risk analysis techniques is explained in a number of textbooks, including the references given at the end of the book and consequently will not be repeated here. Project risk management is not about predicting the future; rather, it is concerned with the identification and effective management of the inherent riskiness of a project option compared with other courses of action, thus enabling and empowering the project manager to make a better decision tomorrow.

No client or project manager wishes to acquire a poor reputation for coping with risk as a result of projects failing to meet deadlines and cost targets. When significant overruns occur on project cost estimates and programs, the effect on the overall project can vary. It will, as a minimum, lessen the project's chances of successfully achieving its objectives. In extreme cases, time and cost overruns can invalidate the economic case for a project, turning a potentially profitable investment into a loss-making adventure.

The terms *risk* and *uncertainty* are frequently used interchangeably but do have different meanings. Risk is usually defined as the adverse effect of an event, which can be associated with a probability of occurrence, and uncertainty is a genuine unknown, which could have adverse or beneficial effects. This chapter considers the management of the effects of both risk and uncertainty.

The purpose of the entire risk management process is to make effective project management decisions about what may happen on the project tomorrow. It has to focus on the future, as the future is the only dimension in which effective change can be made. Yesterday has already happened, and today things are in progress. Therefore, effort must be concentrated on actions and decisions that affect things from the present and onward until the termination of the project.

The Role of the Project Manager in Risk Management

It is the responsibility of the client to undertake risk management, possibly through an appointed project manager, or in the case of a concession contract (discussed in Chapter 7), it would be the promoter's project manager. There is a hierarchical nature to this process, firstly to decide whether the project concept is viable or not; that is, do we proceed or do we abandon? If the decision is made to proceed, then determine whether the project is risky or not; this will be significant in determining basic project strategies like the payment method of the contract and the number of parties involved.

After this comes the feasibility stage when possible options are compared and contrasted to identify the most suitable, and finally risk management can be used by the project manager to manage any threat posed to the achievement of the project objectives—the primary ones being cost, time, and quality.

Project management has a vital role to play through:

- contributing to sound economic appraisal by producing realistic estimates of cost and time related to an appropriate and defined standard of quality
- achieving efficient project implementation through established targets of cost, time, and performance.

In proposed projects, each of the three primary targets of cost, time, and quality might be subject to risk and uncertainty. In terms of project implementation, project managers should undertake or propose actions that reduce or eliminate the effects of risk or uncertainty. They should also ensure that the remaining risks are allocated to the parties in a manner that reflects their ability to manage or control the effects or consequences of risk, and hence be likely to improve project performance.

To achieve these aims it is suggested that a systematic approach be followed.

1. Identify the risk sources.
2. Quantify their effects (risk analysis).
3. Develop management responses to risk.
4. Provide for residual risk in the project estimates (contingencies).

These four stages comprise the process of risk management. Risk management can be one of the most creative tasks of project management. It achieves this through generating realism, thereby increasing commitment to control, and through encouraging problem solving, opening the way to innovative solutions to project implementation.

Risk Management Methodology

The major decisions concerning a project are made early in the project life cycle, at appraisal and sanction stages, respectively. Thus, a realistic estimate of the final cost and duration of the total project is required as early as possible in the life of the project. It therefore follows that all potential risks and uncertainties, which can affect the estimates and act as constraints on the project, should be identified as early as practical in the project's life cycle.

There is a second but equally important reason for the early identification of risks and uncertainties: it focuses project management attention on policies and strategies for the control and allocation of risk, for example, through the choice of an appropriate project strategy and indications of contractual payment types. In particular, it highlights those areas where further design, development work, investigation, or clarification is most needed.

Risk identification can be of considerable benefit, even if the next stage of risk analysis is not undertaken. The constructive nature of this exercise is worth emphasizing, since it is in direct contrast to the notion, sometimes expressed by public relations departments or marketing personnel, that attention to risk creates undue pessimism.

It is important to distinguish the sources of risk from their effects. Ultimately, all risk encountered in project implementation affects one or all of the three primary project targets in terms of failure to keep within the cost estimate, to achieve the required completion date, to achieve the required quality. The main problem is how to identify risks. Three main approaches are adopted, and often all three may be used on a single project. Brainstorming among the project staff is a valuable tool and operates in a similar way to the value management facilitated workshop. Historic projects and data can be consulted, but these are unlikely to be identical and are by definition outdated. Hence, technology and methods may have changed sufficiently to eliminate some risk sources but introduce

Client/Government/Regulatory Agencies
Funding/Fiscal
Definition of Project
Project Organization
Design
Local Conditions
Permanent Plant Supply
Construction Contractors
Construction Materials
Construction Labor
Construction Plant
Logistics
Estimating Data
Inflation
Exchange Rates
Force Majeure

Table 9.1   Major Categories of Sources of Risk

new sources. Finally, risk-source checklists are produced by some industry institutions and learned societies.

As an example, a list of major categories of sources of construction risk is given in Table 9.1. An example for the design risk category is shown in Table 9.2. It is suggested that it would be useful for project managers to develop their own detailed lists appropriate for the type of projects with which they are usually concerned.

After identification, it is necessary to consider those risks with both a high impact on the project and with a high probability of occurrence. If there are none, then the project risk management might go no further. Usually there are some risks of this type, and it is necessary to try to quantify the effect of these risks in more detail.

The purpose of risk analysis is to quantify the effects on the project of the risks identified. The first step is to decide which analytical technique to use. At the simplest level, each risk may be treated independently of all others with no attempt made to quantify any probability of occurrence. Greater sophistication can be achieved by incorporating probabilities and interdependence of risks into the calculations, but the techniques then become more complex. The choice of technique will usually be constrained by the

Adequacy to Meet Need
Experience/Competence of Design Organization

Effectiveness of Coordination
          between design offices
          between contractor's design and client/consultant design

Degree of Novelty

Appropriateness of Design
          to logistics and access
          to climate
          to maintainability
          to operability

Realism of Demands on Construction
Soundness of Design Data

Realism of Design Program
          to design resources
          to construction needs
          to special requirements

Likelihood of Design Change

Table 9.2   Discrete Sources of Risk: Design

available experience, expertise, and computer software (as discussed in Chapter 13).

Whichever technique is chosen, the next step requires that judgments be made of the impact of each risk, and in some cases of the probability of occurrence of each risk, and of various possible outcomes of the risk.

Elementary Risk Analysis

At the simplest level, the individual major risk categories can be aggregated into two or three global risk effects, and a subjective but experienced judgment can be made of their effect on cost and time. This may be adequate when comparing alternatives at the appraisal stage for a well-known type of project. Despite its obvious shortcomings, it is quick, cheap, and provides the project manager with a basis for continuing or discontinuing the analysis.

Sensitivity Analysis

The basis of a sensitivity analysis is to define a likely range of variation for elements of the project data and to measure the consequences of the change in terms of a project variable, for example project cost, net present value, or internal rate of return. In effect, a series of *what-if* estimates are produced.

The results of sensitivity analyses are often presented as a square graph, which readily indicates, by the gradient of the lines, the most sensitive or critical variables toward which management should direct its attention. The closer a variable line is to the project variable axis, the more sensitive the individual variable, because a small change in the individual variable results in a large change in the project variable.

One weakness of sensitivity analysis is that the risks are treated individually and independently, both of which are unlikely to be true in practice. Another weakness is that the method takes no account of the probability of occurrence; although this is less serious because the probability will have been used to reach this stage, and if required probability contours can be added to the sensitivity diagram. Caution must therefore be exercised when using the data directly to assess the effects of combinations of risk.

It may be that none of the identified risks is sensitive, and the analysis can be stopped at this stage. However, if there are any sensitive variables, then a more sophisticated analysis needs to be undertaken.

Probability Analysis

Probability analysis is a more sophisticated form of risk analysis. It overcomes the weaknesses of sensitivity analysis by specifying a probability distribution for each risk, and then considering all the risks in combination. The *Monte Carlo* simulation is the most common approach; it uses a random number generator to sample the probability distributions for each of the key variables on each iteration prior to calculating a project value, usually net present value (NPV) at internal rate of return. Since the outcome from the Monte Carlo analysis is a collection of, say, one thousand values of each evaluation criterion, it is unlikely that the same value for the evaluation criterion will be calculated more than a small number of times. The values are therefore grouped into class intervals. The results are presented as frequency and cumulative frequency distributions of iterations against project value.

Computer packages using a Monte Carlo simulation will produce results in tabular and graphical format; often it is preferable to show output in graphical rather than tabular format. The cumu-

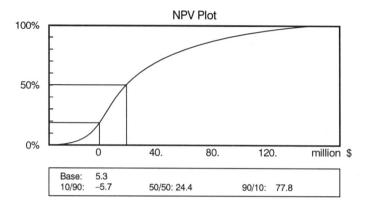

Figure 9.1   Cumulative Frequency Diagram

lative frequency curve is usually illustrated by an S-curve, showing all possible outcomes from 0 to 100 percent (sometimes shown as 0 to 1) along the x-axis, and risk level as measured by a project variable, in this case NPV, along the y-axis.

It is useful to consider Figure 9.1 carefully to understand what is being shown. Many analysts like to make a quick check on the 50 percent out-turn, also known as the 50/50 estimate, which in the case above is $24.4 million. By finding the zero point on the y-axis, the probability of a negative NPV can be found, in this case 20 percent.

Most useful is the range of likely outcomes that can be obtained from the Figure 9.1. These values are not deterministic predictions of the likely performance of the project. The range, which is a function of the gradient of the S-curve, is a direct measure of the inherent riskiness of the project option modeled and can be used to compare with other project options. The range taken for measurement is also the basis of discussion. In the United States and some other countries, the range is usually taken from 10 to 90 percent. In this case, that would equate to a pessimistic NPV (10/90) of -$5.7 million, while the optimistic NPV (90/10) is $77.8 million. In the United Kingdom, the range tends to be between 15 and 85 percent, which would result in outcomes from -$3.1 million to $75.6 million, giving a slightly tighter range. For comparison, all project options should be compared over the same range.

The real value in this type of diagram lies not in reading off the scale but in comparing the cumulative frequency curve for one option with that of another. The steeper the gradient of the curve, the narrower the range, the more certainty is associated with the project. Also, the further along the axis the curve lies, the more profitable, or, in some competitive situations, the less unprofitable the option is likely to be. This is often the summary figure used in technical reports to boards of directors or shareholders and might also be useful in discussions with project sponsors.

Management of Residual Project Risk

Risk response can be considered in terms of avoidance or reduction, transfer or retention.

Avoidance or Reduction

In the extreme, risks may have such serious consequences as to warrant a reappraisal of the project, or even the replacement of the project by an alternative project. It is perhaps more likely that risk identification and analysis will indicate the need for redesign, more detailed design, further site investigation, different packaging of the work content, alternative project strategies, or different methods of implementation in order to reduce or avoid risk.

Transfer

The four most common routes for the transfer of risk in construction projects and contracts are:
- client to contractor or designer
- contractor to subcontractor
- client, contractor, subcontractor, or designer to insurer
- contractor or subcontractor to surety.

The essential characteristic of the transfer response is that the consequences of the risks, if they occur, are shared with or totally carried by a party other than the client. The client should expect to pay a premium for this privilege. The responsibility for initiating this form of risk response therefore lies with the client, and the client should ensure that it is in their best interest to transfer the risk. This will necessitate consideration of both the clients' own and the other parties' objectives, the relative abilities of the parties to assume the risk, the degree of control over the situation, potential gain or loss, and incentive.

Chapter 6 on project strategy contains information on the use of the payment mechanism, and ultimately contract strategy to transfer risk. The maxim to be adopted is that it is only reasonable to transfer risks to parties who are able to control or manage these risks; otherwise high premiums will be incurred.

Retention

Risks that are retained by either party to a contract may be controllable or uncontrollable by that party. Where control is possible, it may be exerted to reduce the likelihood of occurrence of a risk event and also to minimize the impact if the event occurs.

Once the outcome of the analysis has been obtained or *translated*, it remains for the project manager to make the decision, in conjunction with other relevant project information. The risk decision, which is made on the basis of little certain knowledge and the prospect of high impact on the project, is the most difficult to make. This decision is usually *the* most important.

One traditional method used extensively in the engineering and construction industries has been to include time and/or cost contingencies, at varying degrees of accuracy, within the project estimates at each of the project phases.

Understanding the Human Aspects

Risk management is not about predicting the future; consequently, there can be problems describing project risk to management, and convincing others that the project budget should be increased to spend money today to avoid risks that may happen in the future. This emphasizes that the success of practical risk management depends upon human and organizational factors such as understanding, motivation, attitude, culture, and experience.

The quality of project risk management relies on a number of factors, including:
- management attention
- motivation and insight among project personnel
- qualifications and knowledge within the project
- experience and personality of the risk analyst(s) leading the process.

These four key success factors are directly related to people or to how the project organization works. Again, one of the keys for succeeding in risk management is to understand people and their behavior in different roles. (This aspect of project management is addressed in Chapter 10, and this section should be read in conjunction with the principles outlined therein.)

At home as well as at work, everyday choices are affected by risk, and people constantly perform some kind of risk management when making decisions, often without being consciously aware of the process. Crossing busy streets, getting married, and buying a house are all personal risks that most people face. The order of magnitude of the risk decision might increase substantially, and the level of complexity may be much higher in a project risk management decision. It seems much more a problem or challenge to include and perform risk management within the *limits* of a business or industry project.

One of the most important factors in the first stage of the risk management process is the gathering of key personnel to *brainstorm* the identification of risk sources affecting project parameters. The group will most commonly include experts from various disciplines with interfaces to contributors, if known and likely supply chain members, as well as government, regulatory, and sometimes representatives from the local community. A facilitator is often used to ensure that the necessary information is collected. After the brainstorming session is over, the project manager, with key members of the project team, should review the outcomes and consider the risks with a high impact on the project and a high likelihood of occurrence.

The next *human* phase in the risk management process is the communication and understanding of the results achieved from analyzing the risk model. The technical aspects of the risk modeling and analysis have been described earlier. The results achieved in the *analysis* phase should now be translated into project options and communicated to the project manager. The analysis should be repeated to test the sensitivity of input data, key assumptions, and possible inaccuracies in data. All the time, the results are improving the project manager's understanding of the nature of the project. The project risk management should be continued through the project phases until the level of certainty is sufficient to permit deterministic planning methods to be used as the main basis for decision support.

Chapter Ten

Organizational Forms for Managing Projects

THE BASIC FUNCTION or the fundamental purpose of any organizational structure is to provide coordination within the workflow executed by members of an organization. Owing to the division of labor, different members of an organization fulfill different tasks within the entire workflow. Consequently, differentiation has evolved among the members within the organization, which can be interpreted by space, time, and profession, and they require coordination in order to achieve the desired input of the workflow. At the same time, coordination postulates both authority and responsibility. Thus, the organizational structure is a pattern of the mutual relationships among the contributing people of a workflow because of the division of labor, and it is founded on authority and responsibility.

A certain project result could exert a long-term effect on an organization, while the project itself is a unique and practically irreversible undertaking. As was pointed out in Chapter 2, circumstances of project implementation could seriously vary project by project, even with similar projects. As a corollary, both interdependence and uncertainties vary not only project by project but also phase by phase in the case of a given project. At the same time, client characteristics and primary goals relating to project implementation are also variable.

As each project is a unique undertaking, the same is true of the project team; those who are involved in executing and/or managing projects make up a unique formation, too. Thus, the project team is usually disbanded after having completed the project.

All these circumstances represent challenges for both practitioners and academics. There is a need for principles that help practitioners find the right organizational arrangement in a given project.

This chapter will first introduce organizational solutions that are broadly applied for managing projects. Once these forms are considered, light will be shed on their basic characteristics, as well as on their potential advantages and disadvantages. Then, some principles and their associated coordinating mechanisms will come to the forefront in order that the organizational form(s) for a given project can be developed.

The considerations and approaches for developing a certain organizational structure in a given project highlighted in this chapter are useful for both clients and contributors.

Organizational Forms in the Project Process

There are three different basic organizational structures broadly utilized for managing a single project: linear-functional, project task force, and matrix.

Managing Projects Based on a Linear-Functional Organizational Structure

Utilizing the existing linear-functional structure for managing project implementation in an organization provides the means for different project activities or different tasks to be executed and/or managed by different functional units of the organization. In this respect, a project manager does not have authority over the functional managers. As a corollary, a project manager in such a situation does not have the formal authority to enforce her decisions, while the functional managers have authority only within the boundaries of their functional areas. Thus, none of the functional managers has authority over the project as a whole, and there is no line authority between a project manager and the concerned functional managers. Nevertheless, it is not unusual for the field manager to report to the project manager, especially in capital-investment engineering projects. Figure 10.1 examines these relationships.

Top management, at the same time, has authority over the project manager and over the functional managers, as well. Only top management has formal authority in this organizational arrangement to interfere in the project implementation process and to enforce any decision affecting the project as a whole.

Although the project manager is responsible for her project and while her formal authority over the project is significantly less than her responsibility, owing to the position of project managers in this organizational arrangement, she can exert influence to a considerable extent with respect to top-management decisions regarding project implementation. Since project managers are information centers as well—i.e., centralizing information from functional units regarding the project (see project control in Chapter 8) —they have

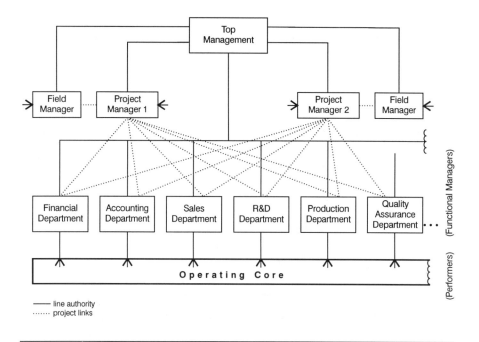

Figure 10.1   Organizational Relationships in Managing Projects Based on a Linear-Functional Structure

the possibility of maintaining an overview about the entire project implementation. They can also fulfill the task of elaborating suggestions for top management in connection with possible decisions pertaining to the project. Although project managers in such a situation are in essence project coordinators, they can exert enormous influence on project implementation.

Those companies using the divisional organizational arrangement also might face the linear-functional structure, when a certain division dealing with a project uses this organizational structure within the division.

Both advantages and disadvantages associated with the project manager's situation can be identified. One possible advantage is that experiences accumulated in a certain functional unit from participation in past projects could be utilized for future projects of the organization. Another advantage is that since the same kind of resources are concentrated into a certain functional unit, the resource utilization could be carried out in a more effective way, even from the point of view of a project.

However, using a linear-functional organizational structure for managing projects could have disadvantages, as well. The following most outstanding disadvantages should be mentioned. In a case where conflicts emerge between a project manager and the functional managers, the project considerations—i.e., the viewpoints of the project as a whole—could be pushed, in general, into the background, in comparison with the functional considerations. There is potential for conflicts since functional managers have not only line authority over a certain segment of the project but also represent interests of the entire organization from a certain functional point of view. Another disadvantage may arise from the fact that a project manager is not a leader of the project implementation in full measure; instead she is a project coordinator with limited formal authority to proceed with the project. In order to cope with possible disadvantages, a project manager in the above situation has to develop a right leadership style and the associated informal, i.e., *de facto*, authority.

Managing Projects with a Project Task Force

A single organizational unit encompassing all those professionals required for managing a project comprises a project task force. In an internal project, those who execute the activities necessary for implementing the project also belong to this separate unit. The project manager in such an arrangement has the power to exercise authority over those belonging to the task force, since the project manager heads the unit. As a consequence, a project manager has the capability to make decisions that relate to implementing the project in accordance with the predefined primary project targets.

It is characteristic to this organizational setting that the task force itself undergoes changes many times during its life cycle, both in terms of number of people and the professions of the members. Changes are carried out according to the needs dictated by the workflow of project implementation. Akin to the linear-functional structure, the project manager also reports to top management, while the task force itself provides the functional units with information regarding the project implementation. Figure 10.2 depicts relationships characteristic to a task-force setting.

Unlike the linear-functional organizational setting, a project manager within a task-force setting has the formal line authority to supervise project implementation and make decisions relevant to it. Thus, a project manager's formal authority and responsibility are in a state of equilibrium. Based on the project managers' situation in this organizational solution, there are both advantages and disadvantages characteristic to any project task-force organizational arrangement.

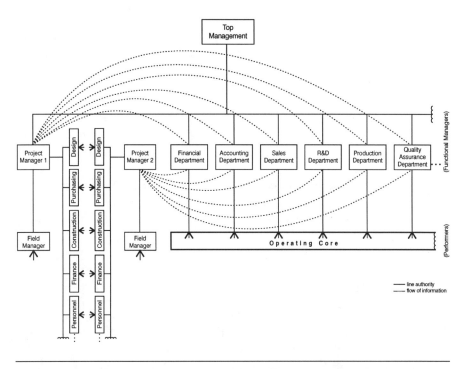

Figure 10.2   Organizational Relationships When Managing Projects with a Project Task Force

The following fundamental possible advantages could be identified. A project task force can be operated with ease either as cost center or profit center. Operating the task force as cost center is characteristic of client organizations; operating as profit center is characteristic of external contributors' organizations. Another advantage is that a project task force integrates the necessary resources into a single organizational unit under a single formal authority. Thus, the task-force organizational arrangement has the potential to concentrate all of the necessary efforts for implementing a single project result.

A task-force setting has potential for the following disadvantages during the course of its application. When conflicts emerge between a project manager and the functional managers, who promote functional standpoints for the entire organization, the functional or professional considerations could be pushed, in general, into the background, in comparison with the project considerations. Also, the task force as an organizational unit is, more or less, in a state of change. Changes regarding the number of members occur, not only with the members' professions but also with their ages, experiences, attitudes, and so on. The potential for establishing a permanent project culture is therefore lessened. Another potential disadvantage lies in the fact that, since the task force is finally disbanded after completing the project, a considerable amount of the experiences accumulated during the course of implementing a given project will not be utilized for future projects.

Coping with disadvantages also necessitates developing the right project-managerial leadership style and proper documentation of the project events.

Managing Projects with a Matrix Organizational Structure

Matrix structures as organizational forms rely on the division of authority between project managers and functional managers. Project activities and their different tasks are carried out by the functional units but, unlike the pure linear-functional and project task-force organizational forms, both project managers and functional managers have formal authority over the project implementation workflow. Similar to the two previously mentioned organizational arrangements, in a matrix structure, both functional and project managers report to top management. Figure 10.3 illustrates the typical relationships characteristic to a matrix structure.

The earlier-mentioned division of authority between the functional and project managers does not imply any line authority between the two groups of managers. Instead, both functional and project managers have the same level of authority over the operating core pertaining to a given project. Therefore, the position of a project manager is dissimilar to any of the formerly mentioned organizational arrangements.

To enhance maintaining operability of a matrix, it is wise for project managers to exercise their authority with respect to the questions of *what to do* and *when* or *by when to do*, while functional managers can exercise authority regarding *how to do* and *who to do*. Nevertheless, to enhance operability, functional and project managers have to come to an agreement in connection with each of these questions. In many cases, this agreement is a result of compromise. Reaching sustainable compromises requires not only the same level of formal authority, but also taking the responsibilities accordingly.

It is a serious hindrance to operability if the functional and project managers are not able to come to an agreement regarding certain questions and instead shift the responsibility of making decisions onto top management. The higher the number of such cases during implementation of a given project, the less potential for operability of the matrix structure. Thus, only significant problems

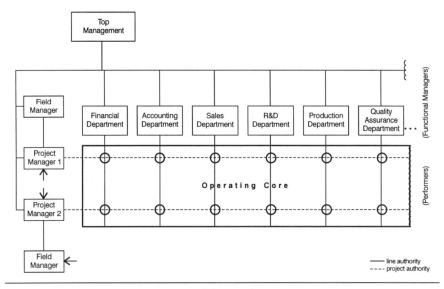

Figure 10.3   Organizational Relationships in Managing Projects Within a Matrix Structure

should be forwarded to top management, accompanied by an analysis of possible alternatives and their consequences.

The matrix structure as an organizational form tries to utilize the potential advantageous characteristics of the linear-functional and the task-force settings, while it tries to minimize the possible disadvantages of them. At the same time, matrices have their own advantageous and disadvantageous characteristics; the following important advantages are inherent in this organizational arrangement.

Akin to the project task force, a matrix also can be operated either as cost center or profit center. The center in this case is the project manager and her staff. Also, the matrix structure offers a further possibility to provide coordination for a project implementation workflow that is not standardized.

At the same time, a matrix organization may have the following significant disadvantages. Operability of a matrix arrangement heavily relies on the organizational culture and the personal characteristics of the members, such as attitudes, communication skill, and so on. The lack of clearly communicated and fairly accepted values in the entire organization creates a potential for conflicts between functional and project managers. Thus, problems are shifted onto top management when it should be concerned with strategy rather than daily problems of a project.

It can be seen that the matrix structure is basically similar to a balanced matrix, which is in some in-between category from a certain point of view. Along with the balanced matrix, both functional (a weak matrix) and project (a strong matrix) matrices are in use. In a weak or functional matrix, the project manager is concerned with coordinating activities of people who are involved in his project. A project manager has the authority pertaining to *by when to do* rather than a definite *when to do*, and he has authority to some degree regarding *what to do*. In a strong project matrix, functional managers provide the project with resources, and at the same time they provide consultation. Thus, the project manager has authority regarding *what to do*, *(by) when to do*, and *how to do* and *who to do*, to a certain degree.

Taking into consideration the characteristics of the above-mentioned models of the matrix structure, it could be stated that the functional matrix comes nearest the linear-functional structure, while the project matrix is closest to the project task force. Thus, the different solutions of the matrix structure create a kind of continuity between managing projects by a linear-functional structure and with the project task force. Nevertheless, this arranging is correct with regard to the scope of formal authority of a project manager only.

Coordinating Mechanisms

Before proceeding with developing the right organizational structure for a given project, the underlying coordinating mechanisms will first be discussed. As was highlighted at the beginning of this chapter, there is a need for coordination because of the differentiation among the members of an organization to achieve the expected outcome of a given workflow. It was also pointed out that differentiation has evolved on the grounds of the division of labor, and the related differentiation could be manifested by space, time, and/or profession.

Spatial differentiation occurs when contributing people of a certain workflow act in different places in order to contribute to the same outcome. Similarly, differentiation by time occurs among people when they act to contribute to the outcome of a certain workflow more or less sequentially. Finally, differentiation by profession occurs when contributing people of a given workflow have different skills. Needless to say, there is some interrelationship among the three types of differentiation on the one hand and between the above-mentioned differentiation and interdependence, especially the workflow interdependence, on the other hand. Thus, it can be said that achieving the desired outcome of any workflow without coordination would be a fortunate accident; consequently,

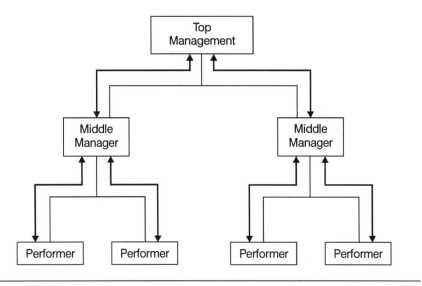

Figure 10.4   Direct Supervision as Coordinating Mechanism

providing coordination is the main function of the organizational structures. Coordination is brought about by means of different coordinating mechanisms.

Two basic types of coordination have evolved in the practice of managing activities: direct supervision and mutual adjustment. Achieving coordination through direct supervision involves one person, based on authority given by the superiors, taking the responsibility of acting as a supervisor to the others working on the task—giving instructions to them and monitoring their work. Members of this group talk about their activities with the person who has line authority over them. Thus, this type of coordination is characterized by basically vertical relationships between a leader and each of her subordinates, not excluding some communication among subordinates. Relationships characteristic to the direct-supervision coordinating mechanism are depicted in Figure 10.4.

Bringing about coordination by using the tool of mutual adjustment relies on communication occurring between people who work on the same task. As a result, this type of coordination, unlike direct supervision, is characterized by a basically horizontal relationship among those who are involved in a workflow. Of course, these prevailing relations pertaining to the execution used for a certain task do not exclude the line authority between superiors and

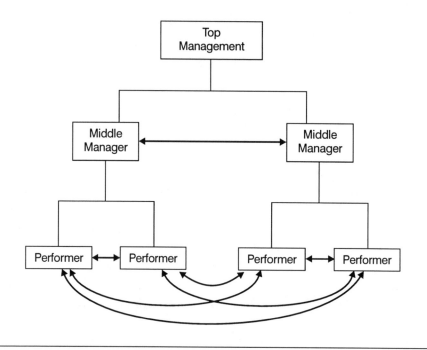

Figure 10.5   Mutual Adjustment as Coordinating Mechanism

subordinates. Figure 10.5 depicts the relationships characteristic to the coordinating mechanism of mutual adjustment.

Direct supervision basically relies on a vertical mode of communication along with the reporting links, while mutual adjustment basically depends on a horizontal method of communication among the people working on a certain task at a certain level of the hierarchy. At the same time, it is also noticeable that at the higher levels of an organizational hierarchy, the mutual adjustment moves more and more to the forefront in comparison with the lower levels in the same organization. This is due to the different nature of activities done, say, at the level of senior executives or at the level of the operating core.

It should be noted here that Mintzberg (1983) considers standardization to be a coordinating mechanism, too. He has identified three types: standardization of the work process, of the inputs, and of the outputs. Although standardization has a decisive role in achieving effective coordination, it is not an immediate coordinating mechanism.

It also has to be noted that the standardization of information as a special kind of input could be very important with regard to coordination, as well. In this respect, the information content itself and the method of information flow are decisive.

Nevertheless, a decision-maker should face the question whether one of the coordinating mechanisms is the most sound in the case of a given workflow. In order to find the right answer, one should go back to the phenomena of interdependence and uncertainty characteristics to a workflow. It is then self-evident that the lower the complexity of the workflow interdependence characteristics and the lower the number and intensity of the uncertainties characteristic to a specific workflow, the higher the possibility for standardizing the workflow and the related inputs and outputs. As a consequence, coordination could be achieved by direct supervision. Based on the standards associated with both workflow and related input and output, a manager can give instructions with ease to subordinates and can exercise control over their work in the same way.

Otherwise, when complex interdependence and/or many uncertainties of high intensity characterize the workflow, there is no potential for standardization. Thus, there is a need for mutual adjustment in order to achieve the necessary coordination. In such a situation, a manager is not in a position to give clear instructions for the subordinates separately from each other.

What are the consequences of the above-mentioned interrelations with respect to the organizational structures? In the workflow, which can be standardized because of its characteristics, a one-dimensional linear-functional organizational structure can provide coordination, since this organizational arrangement utilizes direct supervision as a coordinating mechanism. In such a case, the scalar chain—i.e., the number of levels in the hierarchy—and the span of control—i.e., the number of subordinates reporting to a certain manager—can be increased to a certain extent without impeding effective coordination, in accordance with the measure of standardization.

Otherwise, if the workflow in question cannot be standardized because of the related characteristics, there could be a need, say, for a two-dimensional matrix structure, since the one-dimensional linear-functional organizational setting cannot provide coordination. Matrix structures utilize, because of the division of authority, mutual adjustment as a coordinating mechanism. In such a case, both scalar chain and span of control should be decreased for the sake of effective coordination. Owing to the high number of uncertainties and the complex workflow interdependence, enforcing coordination by using direct supervision in the frame of a linear-functional structure would result in slowing the pace of implementation because of the relatively longer scalar chain. These interrelationships are outlined in Figure 10.6.

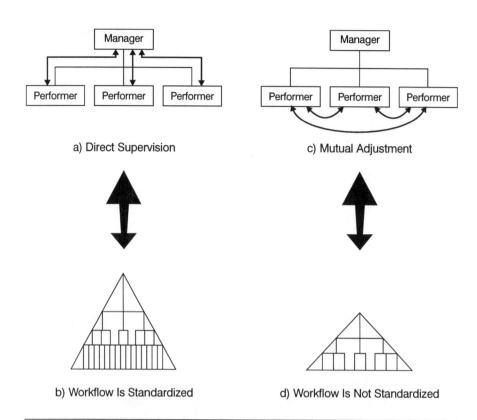

a) Direct Supervision

c) Mutual Adjustment

b) Workflow Is Standardized

d) Workflow Is Not Standardized

Figure 10.6   Interrelationships between Characteristics of the Workflow and the Pyramids of the Organization

Considering interrelationships existing between the characteristics of the workflow, the appropriate coordination, and the related organizational structure, it should be highlighted that in finding the right organizational arrangement, the role of scale interdependence also could be decisive. In a small organization, which has a few employees only, the complexity of workflow interdependence is low, and there are no significant uncertainties in the workflow. Thus, the workflow itself can be standardized with ease; effective coordination could be achieved by mutual adjustment rather than by using direct supervision. A small car-repair shop could be a case in point.

Developing the Right Structure

Up to this point, differentiation of the organizational structures utilized for managing projects has been based on the scope of formal authority of project managers possessing the different organizational forms. When the question of developing the right structure in a given project arises, a need for another differentiation results. Since the fundamental function of the organizational structures is to provide coordination, it seems logical to differentiate by organizational forms, based on their coordinating capacity with respect to the project implementation workflow.

Coordinating capacity is the least consideration in the linear-functional structure, since all three kinds of differentiation can be found among the members of such an organization. In a project task force, there is no spatial differentiation in terms of organizational units; all of the members belong to the same task force. Thus, there is a potential for utilizing the mutual adjustment also for coordinating project activities within the task force. In this way, the rigidity of the differentiation by time could be smelted. As a corollary, the coordinating capacity of a project task force is considerably greater than that of the linear-functional structure. Nonetheless, scale interdependence—i.e., the extent and the complexity of the project— could set limits to the coordinating capacity of a project task force.

When a big multifunction project is considered, such as the Olympic Games or a world exhibition, the extent and complexity of the project necessitates a big functionally structured multilevel task force to manage project implementation. All three kinds of differentiation will appear again, but within the organizational boundaries of the project task force; in this way, the coordinating capacity of this task force is similar to that of a linear-functional structure. Thus, there is a need for an organizational setting that has greater coordinating capacity than a project task force, in general. Owing to the division of authority between functional and project managers, and the associated mutual adjustment, this structure is the two-dimensional matrix organization.

Based on existing interrelationships between project implementation workflow characteristics and realizable standardization, interrelationships between suitable types of coordinating mechanisms and the appropriate organizational structure, and differentiation pertaining to the integrative capacity of organizational forms, the right organizational structure can be found for a given project. The higher the complexity of the interdependence characteristic to the workflow, and the greater the intensity and the number of uncertainties in the workflow, the stronger the need for an organizational structure that has greater integrative capacity. Managing project implementation with a linear-functional structure could be effective in such a case if the related workflow could be satisfactorily standardized. Due to standardization, there is no need for interference from top management. Bear in mind that in a linear-functional structure, only top management has the authority to interfere in the project as a whole; however, too much interference will restrain the pace of implementation.

The workflow creating different types of project results can be standardized to different extents. Thus, in general, different projects require dissimilar organizational structures. Since the phases of the project cycle encompass different activities, developing the right organizational form for a given project requires a more sophisticated approach.

More complex interdependence and numerous uncertainty factors characterize the preparation phase for any project, regardless of the type of the project. Thus, standardization could hardly be achieved to a satisfactory extent. In most cases, there is a need for a project task force to achieve effective coordination. There could be a need for some model of the matrix structure for a big multifunctional project, such as an international airport.

The awarding phases of projects show many similarities to project preparation. Thus, the consequences relating to the organizational structures are more or less the same. There could be significant dissimilarities even with the same type of project within the implementation phase of the project cycle. The implementation workflow for a capital investment-engineering project can generally be standardized because of the quantifiability of these projects. Thus, in most cases, the required coordination is achieved by utilizing the linear-functional structure. At the same time, the implementation phase of an R&D project or an intellectual-service project cannot be standardized to an acceptable extent. Consequently, effective coordination requires a project task force or some matrix structure in general, depending on the scale interdependence characteristic to the project.

As an ultimate consequence, it can be stated that changing the organizational form utilized for a given project in accordance with the varying project characteristics is considered to be a normal practice rather than a unique whim. Nevertheless, besides the above-mentioned interrelationships, the following circumstances could exert some influence on making decisions relating to the organizational structure:

- whether the organization as a whole has the appropriate functional units
- whether the functional units of the entire organization are capable of dealing with projects, as well as with their daily activities.

These circumstances can alter the previously introduced pure organizational forms, and shortages relating to the circumstances could lead to developing a mutant of the pure forms. Applying these variants is not necessarily a hindrance to effective coordination. A frequently applied solution involves people whose work is needed for the project full time being involved in a task force, while those who are engaged in the project on a part-time basis work under the authority of the functional managers, coordinated by the project manager.

Looking back to the BÓRA Co.'s Old Country Project (see Chapter 6), we recall that the following factors exerted influence when developing an organizational arrangement for the project implementation phase came to the forefront:

- interdependencies and uncertainties characteristic to the implementation phase
- expertise and capacity of the existing functional units
- concomitants of the type of contract used in the project strategy.

Based on the uncertainties and interdependencies characteristic to the project implementation phase (see Figure 6.3), the workflow was considered fairly standardized; therefore, achieving the required coordination is possible through the use of the existing linear-functional structure. Considering the expertise and capacity of these functional units, it can be said that neither the expertise previously accumulated nor the present capacity of the functional units would provide effective coordination. At the same time, the type of contract applied to the project implementation, i.e., the management type, does not require too many people in the client's organization being involved. As a corollary, a small task force was established, and most of the members were hired from outside, while a few functional executives supported the project on a part-time basis.

When making decisions about organizational forms, the project manager should be considered, too. In each of the three mentioned organizational forms, one finds three project managers possessing three different scopes of formal authority. A project manager's formal authority derives from top management; this is the power that provides the opportunity for project managers to act on the one hand and provides limits for them on the other hand. This power in the hands of a project manager is referred to as *de jure* authority. Most important is the actual authority of a project manager, which is referred to as *de facto* authority. De jure authority is only one component of de facto authority; the latter depends on different personal qualities of the project manager, such as professional skills, communication skills, experiences, empathy, and so on. Yet, one of the most decisive factors shaping de facto authority is the leadership style characteristic to a project manager. The earlier-mentioned personal qualities also could shape leadership style. (It is not the intention of the authors to give a full-scale snapshot of the phenomenon; we only want to highlight the problem.)

The leadership style of a project manager, akin to other managers, can vary between two extremes: human orientation and task orientation. Between these two extremes, there could be a number of combinations. In a stable environment, as in industrial mass production, for example, an appropriate combination can be identified with relative ease. In a turbulent project environment, regarding the project cycle even for a single project, there is a need for a sophisticated balance between human and task orientation. A project manager should be able to modify leadership style appropriately in a given situation in accordance with the changing project environment.

Developing the ability to achieve sound use of leadership style and the concomitant de facto authority could be decisive for project managers, especially when a project manager has very limited formal authority, as with the linear-functional structure or a functional matrix. An appropriate or adequate leadership style could substitute for the missing de facto authority.

Up to this point, only application of different organizational structures within a single project has been discussed. Because of the variety of strategic objectives in an organization, there could be a number of projects within the entire organization at the same time. Thus, there is a need for coordination between projects as well, and this should be reflected in the organizational arrangement of the entire organization. (Of course, there is a need for coordination, especially with respect to resources and between project and non-project activities, too. However, this coordination is not discussed in this book.) The associated considerations have led to the project-oriented organizations. (The approaches may be applied by both client organizations and contributors participating in a few projects simultaneously.)

In a project-oriented organizational arrangement, a new position appears, namely project director or manager of project managers. An outline of the project organization is depicted in Figure 10.7.

The conception of the project-oriented organizational arrangement is applicable regardless of the organizational structures utilized for each project in the organization as a whole. The manager of project managers, i.e., the project director, has authority over project managers in any case.

A project director in a project-oriented organization should fulfill, with respect to his responsibility and authority, the following most important tasks.

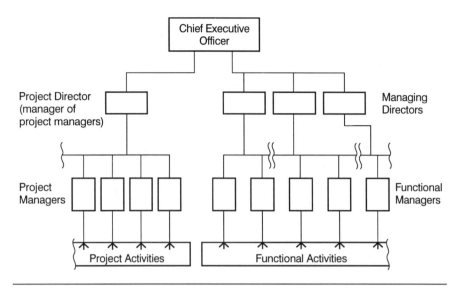

Figure 10.7   Relationships in a Project-Oriented Organization

- Transform strategic objectives into projects, including different versions of the project ideas.
- Provide coordination between projects with respect to timing, resource allocation, and cost estimation.
- Match strategic objectives and projects under implementation.
- Accept (or refuse) completed project results.
- Exercise control over projects and project managers.

The idea of a project-oriented organizational setting is also utilized in superprojects or megaprojects. When managing implementation of a megaproject, it could become necessary to split up the entire project and form subprojects. During the course of shaping the subprojects, the rules of thumb introduced in Chapter 6 pertaining to elaborating work packages in a traditional-type contract should be applied.

Each of the subprojects should have an independent manager reporting to a main project manager, who also could be referred to as a project director. This person fulfills the same tasks attributed to a project director in a project-oriented organizational arrangement.

Chapter Eleven

Understanding Project Success

MOST OF THE literature concerned with project success has a narrow outlook. The common approach to analyzing project success is through use of statistical methods supported by empirical data. These statistical methods have revealed many success and failure factors in different types of projects. During the course of the analyses, different baseline and measurement systems have been used for conducting evaluations. Yet, even though these studies have contributed to an understanding of project success in many ways, in general they lack a multidimensional approach to the concept.

In this chapter, a conceptual framework for understanding project success will be revealed instead of presenting techniques and tools for identifying either success or failure factors.

Since projects provide the means for achieving strategic objectives, they enable an organization to perform within a changing environment. Success at the strategic level of a project requires utilization of additional parameters to primary project targets.

These concepts are always difficult to grasp. The Thames Barrier Project in London is an interesting example. The project had technical difficulties with mechanical lock gates; it had contractual difficulties between the parties and funding difficulties between the different sections of government acting as client. The project was completed over budget and over time with many technical changes, and yet it has been used on three occasions since completion to prevent potentially serious flooding in central London. Therefore, is the project a success or a failure, and on what grounds?

To clearly demonstrate the proposed framework and to provide the reader with a better understanding of the process, project success will be interpreted based on primary project targets and organizational strategic objectives and from the point of view of interest groups. After introducing this framework, the implications of success and failure for project managers will also be presented in this chapter.

Project Success at Project Level

The simplest approach to evaluating project success can be carried out using the primary project targets: cost, time, and performance or quality. In this way, if the predefined project out-turns of duration, budget, and performance have been achieved, the project implementation is considered successful.

Sometimes it becomes necessary to make modifications to one or more of the primary project targets during the implementation stage of a project. This situation is not necessarily the result of poor project management. It may rather be attributed to weak scope definition of the project during the project preparation-formation phase; poor time and cost estimates during the project preparation-formation phase; and unforeseeable economic and technical difficulties at the time of project initiation.

Weak project scope definition could occur as a result of insufficiently specified strategic objectives during project initiation because of a lack of expertise in the client's organization regarding both the expected project out-turn and the project formation itself, or due to the novelty of the expected project out-turn. Any of these reasons could result not only in modifications to the primary project targets, but in downstream changes and other consequences during project implementation. Research and development projects are particularly sensitive to this type of disruption.

Low estimates of costs and completion time could stem from weak scope definition or may have been made intentionally. In such a case, those who develop the project proposal are trying to artificially increase the perception of the project. This approach assumes that once a project has been launched, it would not be cancelled. Needless to say, the use of artificially low estimates with regard to either costs or duration times would result in unsuccessful project implementation in the sense adopted in this chapter.

Unforeseeable economic and technical difficulties generally can influence all of the primary project targets during project implementation. Economic difficulties have a direct effect on costs and completion time and, as a corollary, could influence the desired project result, resulting in lower quality, narrower scope, and so on. At the same time, technical difficulties generally exert influences on the expected project result first; therefore, both predefined costs and duration time would be altered. Generally speaking, the more novel either the expected project out-turn or the implementation workflow, the more likely it is that technical difficulties could arise and lead to unsuccessful project implementation.

The Orlyval light rail project in Paris is an example of a project that satisfied its primary project targets by completing a complex engineering project of tunneling through urban Paris and installing a permanent-way rail track within budget, on time, and in accordance with quality standards. Yet, due to operational failures, the project was judged as a commercial failure, based on its inability to pay off the project debt from generated revenue. All in all, interpreting project success at the level of the primary project targets implies that project completion has been realized in accordance with the predefined project triangle, or even better.

Project Success at the Organizational Level

Is project implementation that results in a different project out-turn than the one predefined or in the expected project out-turn being realized over a longer duration and/or at a higher cost than estimated necessarily considered a failure? The answer is: Not necessarily.

The point is whether the completed project has contributed to achieving strategic objectives of the client organization. Thus, matching strategic objectives and completed projects is another approach to evaluating project success. Projects are derived from strategic objectives, which may with time reveal that they were based on defective premises, or they may change with time. Unless such a realization is followed with modification or even cancellation of the relevant project, completing the project in accordance with its original formation is a waste of money. Thus, completion is considered unsuccessful.

Assuming that completion of a certain project is in accordance with the client organization's realistic strategic objectives and that project implementation corresponds to the predefined primary project targets, the following question would arise: Are those groups of people or organizations who have some vested interest in the project as a whole going to accept it or not?

Attitudes of possible interest groups could be decisive with respect to both project success and project failure. These attitudes could lead to rejection of the project out-turn, even after the project has been completed. The Hainburg Atomic Power Station in Austria is a case in point: technologically satisfactory but no longer in keeping with the environmental and safety values of the community. Also, increasing implementation costs in a public project could lead to project cancellation, as was the case with Expo '96 in Hungary.

Modifications or changes represent opportunities for project managers to turn a potential project failure into a project success. A modification emerging during the course of project implementation may be aimed at primary project targets: desired project result, duration time of implementation, and costs of project implementation. Any of these modifications could have some effect on the other primary project targets, depending upon the extent of the change. From the point of view of the projects' success in the sense discussed here, the modifications pertaining to the desired project out-turn are decisive for two reasons, as follows.

■ A desirable and complete project out-turn is directly related to the potential of achieving the strategic objectives of the client organization.
■ Modifications aiming toward the expected project out-turn generally influence both cost and duration time.

Similar to expanding organizational strategy, modifying a project out-turn could be motivated by both external and internal environmental forces. Generally, the following external environmental factors are significant: emerging needs of customers and more beneficial technical solutions; limited capabilities of potential contributors; introduction of new regulations, either international or local; and changing external interest-group attitudes. At the same time, the following internal environmental factors are of great importance:

■ changing strategic objectives and the occasionally concomitant changing of the priority order of the projects within the client organization
■ emerging user and operator demands during project implementation
■ priority assignment for more beneficial solutions
■ changing internal regulations
■ unsolvable technical and/or financial problems
■ unchangeable implementation deadline
■ changing attitudes of internal interest groups.

Although the above listings are comprehensive, they are not prescriptive or exhaustive. When any modification occurs for any reason, it is necessary to follow a formal review procedure. Project control reports generally supply valuable information for considering possible modifications. (Control theory was discussed in greater detail in Chapter 8.)

When strategic objectives in the client organization undergo change, a modification may be necessary because in such a case the priority order of projects may change, the primary targets may change, or the project might be cancelled. Modifications may also be required to evaluate the likely effects of major technical, financial, and other problems, and the likely implications of changing attitudes of the major groups.

The need for canceling a project generally evolves during the course of implementation rather than emerging suddenly because of a single unforeseeable event. Often, canceling a project is preceded by attempts to modify the project. Akin to modifications, cancellation of a project is not necessarily a failure for the entire organization. Although the possibility of a project failure is not excluded at the level of the primary project targets, cancellation should involve strategic considerations.

Learning from practice, the circumstances that could necessitate project cancellation can be identified. The following signals should be considered in this respect:

- considerable change in the client's organizational strategy, e.g., in privatization or merger
- unsolvable technical problems or highly risky technical solutions emerging during project implementation, e.g., in complex and novel R&D projects
- serious time overrun and/or cost overrun.

Although modification or cancellation of a project requires senior management approval, project managers should exert great influence on the outcome, since both project-controlling reports and project-review meetings provide the factual bases upon which a decision will be made.

Implications for Project Managers

Project success or failure depends on a number of different circumstances; however, it should be recognized that many influential factors are within the compass of the client's organization. Thus, one of the most important factors for project success is the client's attitude. David Cleland stresses this statement: "Project owners cannot leave to others the responsibility for continuously measuring the success of the project, even experienced project management contractors and constructors" (1994, 93).

The client is not an abstraction; from the point of view of a project, a project manager represents a client. Human beings are inclined to attribute project failures to the project manager. Although this possibility cannot be excluded, many reasons for project failure are beyond the project manager's control. Nevertheless, when a project manager is appointed, the criteria upon which the project's success is based should be clearly communicated to him. At the same time, criteria for both modification and cancellation are to be communicated, as well. This forms a basis for a structured and systematic approach to understanding project success.

For the sake of project success, a client and/or project manager should fulfill the following fundamental tasks. Clients should make every effort to develop a quantitative full-scale project-scope definition of the desired project out-turn. Elaborating the associated time and cost constraints in the same manner is also beneficial. Matching strategies with the actual primary project targets, especially before decisions are made at the critical decision points in the project cycle, is beneficial. Along with this, matching strategies and the results of the implementation process at the milestones or ramifications also could be decisive in hardly quantifiable or novel R&D projects. Detail a project strategy (type of financial settlement and type of contract) by allocating associated responsibilities and risks in accordance with both project characteristics and client characteristics. At the same time, utilizing the appropriate tendering procedures and the concomitant prequalification criteria is also decisive.

Another fundamental task for a client and/or project manager leading toward project success involves modifying or canceling projects when changes in strategy dictate, even if the projects are under execution. Through continuous project marketing activity, *selling* both the project result to be implemented and the process of project implementation to the interest groups is important. Modifying or canceling projects because of the interest groups' attitudes is also a consideration. Lastly, integrate properly implemented project results with the operating process of the entire organization. In order to fulfill these tasks, a client should consider three rules of thumb:

1. Apply those project management tools and methods that best suit the nature of the project in question; that is, avoid using uniform solutions.

2. Apply a project control system that not only reports the present deviations but also anticipates possible future deviations highlighting the need for potential modification or cancellation.

3. Develop a project culture embedded in the organizational culture. This project culture should involve the shared values of people, and it could be materialized in different ways, e.g., project logo.

Chapter Twelve

Project Marketing

SUCCESSFUL PROJECT IMPLEMENTATION is a goal for both project clients and contributors. Project success, as was pointed out in Chapter 11, is a multifaceted phenomenon shaped by a host of different factors. One of the most decisive factors is project marketing, which can be interpreted both from the points of view of project clients and the contributing organizations.

When a client considers project marketing, emphasis is placed on those groups of people and organizations who have or might have some interest in a specific project. Marketing in this respect can be traced back to the theory of stakeholder management, and those who have or might have interest in a project could be referred to as interest groups. It is important to a project's success whether the different interest groups are going to accept the desired project result (e.g., as in a business-process reengineering project) and the project implementation process (e.g., as in construction of a natural gas network in a city).

Hostile attitudes of the most influential interest groups could result in project failure, while in other cases, they could prompt a reasonable project cancellation. Projects financed by public money or projects that affect the way of life of people are cases in point. The first part of this chapter presents an overview of dealing with possible interest groups.

Project marketing could be considered from the point of view of the external contributors. In this respect, emphasis is placed on those marketing tools applicable in a project environment that enable contributors to sell their capabilities appropriate to implementing certain projects. During project implementation, a client—the buyer—buys not only the expected project result but also a package of services. This service package supplies project management services to a certain extent (mainly depending on the type of contract utilized in the project implementation), and the client is also an active participant in this activity. When prequalification was considered in Chapter 6, it was stated that this package of services could be a decisive criterion of evaluation. W. Murray and H. Moody pointed out that, based on empirical research, many big clients consider the contributors' management service as the most important bid evaluation criteria (1981). The quality of managing project activities, so to say, materializes in the completed project result in terms of duration time, costs, and different parameters that can be utilized subsequently by the contributors as references.

In such a case, it is nearly self-evident that the tools of marketing are different from those of the mass products market. Personal selling comes to the forefront in the project market, while the role of the traditional distribution policy becomes underrated, and so on. At the same time, the structural arrangement of the related activity within the entire organization and the associated flow of information also will be different.

Nevertheless, these are not the marketing tools themselves, which are different in this case, but rather the environment in which the tools are used. Thus, this chapter does not deal with introducing the basics of marketing tools. (P. Kotler presents a reliable overview of marketing tools [1997].) Instead, the basic characteristics of buyers themselves, i.e., project clients, and basic characteristics with respect to decision-making will be introduced, since these are the cornerstones of the possible contributors' marketing activity.

Project Marketing for Project Clients

Project marketing, from the point of view of a client, is such a proactive activity that a client could not only *sell* projects for the interest groups, but also identify expectations and emotions associated with a given project. This would help those who are responsible for managing the project to satisfy the rational demands of the interest groups on the one hand, and to avoid unnecessary conflicts through clear communication on the other hand. With the help of project marketing, the support of the interest groups could be enhanced or, at least, their hostility toward the project could be moderated.

To a client, an interest group could be any community or any other organized or occasional group that has the same or almost the same interest regarding either the project implementation process or the expected project result—for example, the operating life cycle of the project result. Thus, project marketing should be pursued throughout the entire project life cycle.

Behavior of the different interest groups involved in the project, because of their different motivations, could be supporting or hostile; of course, it could be neutral, as well. It is not uncommon for a certain interest group to change its attitude while new previously nonexistent interest groups could emerge during the project life cycle. Furthermore, it is a hindrance to project implementation that the intensity of manifesting interests could be different in groups that have the same attitude. At the same time, it is also frequently noticed that there are dissimilar reasons and interests behind the same attitude. As a result, conflicts could develop not only between the project owner and the hostile interest groups, but also among the interest groups—moreover among those interest groups that have the same attitude in connection with the project in question. The Gabcikovo-Nagymaros hydropower station in Hungary is a case in point.

Owing to the above-mentioned possible situations, there is a real need for project marketing from the outset of a project idea until the end of the project life cycle. Thus, it is wise for the feasibility studies to attach great importance to the possible interest groups.

Formulating the client's attitude to the interest groups is similar in many respects to developing an attitude to the competitors during strategy formulation. Nevertheless, due to the previously mentioned circumstances, the former is more or less a continuous activity, consisting of the following steps.

1. Identify the possible interest groups.
2. Identify the nature and the content of the interests pursued by the groups.
3. Identify the level of organization of the interest groups.
4. Identify the attitudes of the groups to the project implementation and the operating life cycle of the project result.
5. Refine the relevant marketing tools in order to shape the interest groups' attitudes.

Of course, the first two steps could be carried out simultaneously, bearing in mind their interrelationships. For the sake of a clearer picture, they will be considered separately.

Possible interest groups involved in a project can be categorized into two main categories: internal and external. This differentiation is justified by the fact that the internal interest groups, unlike the external groups, exist and act, to a different extent, under the authority of the client organization. The most important internal interest groups are:

- owners and other stockholders of the client organization
- people involved in the projects, either managing the implementation or performing project activities
- users of the expected project result
- other employees, basically differentiated by profession

- client organization managers, differentiated partly by profession but partly by hierarchy
- employee unions.

    Although the internal interest groups exist and act under the authority of the client organization, they do not necessarily support the organization's projects. On the other hand, those people who belong to one of the internal groups could be members of an external interest group, even a group with hostile attitudes toward the project.

    It is also necessary to differentiate the external interest groups, first of all based on their scope of activity. In this respect, the following most important external interest groups could be identified:

- government agencies and authorities, e.g., ministries and/or municipalities
- business-related organizations, e.g., banks providing finance
- trade unions
- professional associations
- customers
- political parties
- movements, e.g., *greens*
- general public
- local communities
- news media.

    Obviously, it cannot be taken for granted that all internal or external interest groups will have any interest in each project. It is also easy to see that a certain interest group could represent the same interest to a different extent with regard to different projects. Nevertheless, categorizing the possible interest groups could help a project client identify the interests represented by those groups related to a certain project.

    Given a project environment and bearing in mind that projects are means of strategy implementation, the following relevant vested interests could be identified:

- economic interest—e.g., owners of the client organization would like to reduce operational cost by means of a business-process reengineering project
- interest granted by law—e.g., a health authority has the legal right to refuse an operating license in a project result, such as for a restaurant
- mission-governed interest—e.g., a motorway construction project directly related to the mission of the green movements
- political interest—e.g., a project that creates jobs
- interest motivated by safety—e.g., employees in a client organization could develop a hostile attitude to a project introducing a computer-based operating process

- interest motivated by survival—e.g., a local community could support a project, since it creates jobs for its members
- interest related to a way of life and health—e.g., projects that could dramatically affect both lifestyle and health opportunities, such as airports.

It is easy to see that a certain interest group could have a couple of conflicting vested interests in any given project. Moreover, the members of a certain group could share different vested interests, as well, in the same project. Thus, from the point of view of a client, identifying the level of organization of those groups that have vested interest in the project could be decisive since, based on this, the client can assess the extent to which a group is able to enforce its vested interest. Needless to say, there could be significant differences between an occasional group of people and a mission-governed, well-established organization.

Analyzing the level of organization should encompass at least two points. First, does the group in question have a clearly communicated mission and strategy to serve as a focus for group activities? Second, what are the group's strengths and weaknesses for realizing the mission and achieving the strategic objectives?

After having completed all of the tasks outlined up to this point, the client should be concerned with the groups' attitudes. Beyond making a distinction between supporting and opposing or neutral groups, the reasons behind the groups' attitudes and the intensity of the expected enforcing of interests also could be evaluated. Especially with regard to hostile groups, analyzing likely modes and forms of enforcement—i.e., the way in which the groups would respond to the project as a whole or to certain events associated with the project—could be of great importance.

The above-mentioned tasks and the implied analyses and evaluations could result in lists of the strongest supporters and the strongest opposing groups. These lists directly lead the client to the task of identifying marketing tools that can shape the groups' attitudes. Before proceeding with these tools, a couple of things should be kept in mind.

As mentioned earlier, although the internal interest groups partly exist and act under the authority of the client organization, their members could join a hostile external group. Thus, in general, the external groups require more attention. Also, since government agencies and authorities exercise legal rights, their responses, apart from borderline cases, are predictable. Therefore, this circumstance does not require the previously introduced series of steps. Remember that the news media plays a peculiar role among the interest groups. While any group can communicate to the media its attitude regarding a given project, on the other hand, the news media, because of its mission, could exercise influence through its information and information resources.

It is also wise to remember that the bigger and the more complex the project is, there is a stronger need for a systematic approach to the interest groups. This is especially true in projects that could violate fundamental rights and interests. Projects financed by public money could be cases in point. Also, it frequently can happen that different interest groups, which have similar attitudes to a certain project, could strengthen each other's attitudes and behaviors. Moreover, the strengthening behavior may result in the emergence of previously nonexistent interest groups.

Considering as a starting point that a certain interest group has basically either a supporting or a hostile attitude to a project, the applicable marketing tools and the mode of applying them can be shaped by the characteristics of the groups with any vested interest in the project; the nature of the vested interest of the related groups; and the expected manner of enforcement exercised by the interest groups. Thus, certain tools are used to help project clients elaborate their project marketing considerations: consultative meetings, involvement, and different communication tools.

Consultative meetings may be organized, especially during the project preparation phase, when interest groups have interest in a project that is granted by law. Most of the authorities fall under this category.

Involvement in the project preparation by those employees who are to be the users of the expected project result is useful for demolishing resistance and reinforcing support. Inviting the interest groups to participate in the project start and the project closure meetings is also a kind of involvement. Information technology projects are cases in point.

As for communication tools, communication itself could be used in different ways: the news media; regularly circulated leaflets about the project and the project implementation, highlighting results gained; symposiums and/or site visits organized for the interest groups.

It could be generally stated that most project marketing tools are applicable to a certain degree with any interest group and with any vested interest. Thus, a mix of marketing tools should be developed for any given project, which will enable a client to keep the interest groups informed about every aspect of a project and respond to any piece of news or rumor emerging on the project.

Project Marketing for Contributors

Project marketing in this sense is akin to the usual meaning of the word *marketing*. Therefore, in this respect, project marketing provides a means for promoting the business activity of a possible contributor. In comparison with the market of mass products, the environmental factors are basically different in the project market. Tools involved in the marketing mix as framework are applied in a different environment. The most important part of this environment is the client decision-making process. Thus, the rest of this chapter will deal with those factors that are most decisive to a client's decision-making, namely:

- basic characteristics of the project market and the project client as buyer
- basic characteristics of a client's decision-making with respect to *buying* a project result
- factors that could shape, in general, client decision-making when buying a certain project result.

Basic Characteristics of the Project Market and the Project Client as Buyer

In the project market, similar to other markets, a possible contributor should face different market positions. The expected market positions can range from the perfect competition, through the oligopoly, to the monopoly. The market position of a contributor could change dramatically project by project. The situation is explained by the following conditions. First, the geographic distance of the contributor's resources from the site of project implementation could exert a serious impact on his market position. The greater this distance, the closer the perceived market position is to the monopolistic one for a contributor. Thus, the oligopoly is frequently imperfect, and, as with the monopoly, it offers only a temporary advantage to win a certain contract.

Second, the type of contract applied for project strategy could be decisive. Moving from the traditional type of contract toward the turnkey-type contract, the perceived market position of a possible contributor more and more could resemble the oligopoly and finally the monopoly. On the other hand, those project strategies that utilize some arrangement of the traditional contract could create a nearly perfect competition for the contributors.

Last, the capability of a possible contributor in the mirror of the previously mentioned conditions could shape the perceived market position of a contributor, as well. The better the capabilities of a contributor for a specific project, the more monopolistic his perceived market position regarding the project is.

Nevertheless, the phenomenon of monopsony also could occur, especially in the defense industry where the only buyer, the client, is the central government. Clients as buyers have pivotal roles in this market, since not only the need for a certain project result arises in their organization, but the primary decisions affecting implementation are also made in the client organization. As projects could be very dissimilar, their clients also may be different. Clients could be grouped, based on different criteria such as their businesses, whether they are profit oriented or not, and so on. With regard to project marketing in the sense put down at the outset, grouping of the clients based on forms of ownership looks sound. It is verified by the fact that clients are organizational buyers, and their decision-making processes and mechanisms are basically shaped by the form of ownership. Based on this criterion, the following types of client can be identified: individual, corporate, and public. The same grouping of clients was used by A. Walker (1989).

The *individual client* as buyer is relatively rare and found mainly in privately owned small companies. The only owner is the person maintaining direct connection with the contributors, although employees are not necessarily excluded from the decision-making process. Nonetheless, the owner keeps the right to make decisions and, as a corollary, the decision-making mechanism becomes simple and easy to survey, and the process itself is shortened.

The *corporate client* is the buyer when decisions are made in a body. These clients have a multilevel complex organizational structure, consisting of a number of different units, which is involved in the decision-making process to different extents. The participants' capabilities to exert influence on the outcome of the decision-making process are dissimilar, depending partly on the formal assignment of the persons and partly on their informal status. These circumstances require that the possible contributors become acquainted with the client's organizational structure and the relevant decision-making mechanism. In connection with this, a contributor should identify those units and persons that could exert influence on the outcome of the decision-making process to the greatest extent. In the course of this marketing activity, these units and persons would become target groups, and the possible contributors should persuade them to influence decision-making, based on the strengths of each specific contributor. Approaching a client in this way could become more complicated when the client belongs to a group of companies.

The *public client* as buyer has many similarities in common with the corporate client. In general, public clients are government agencies and municipalities. State-owned companies in a market economy share many similarities with privately owned companies; thus, they could be considered as corporate clients in this respect. A significant difference between corporate and public clients is that most of the corporate clients not only operate the completed project result, but many of them have business connections with the users and the consumers. Generally, a public client, even if she operates the completed project result, in most cases is not in business connection with the users. In many cases, the financial resources for a public project are granted by the central budget and, as a result, the donor would exercise a certain control over the project. At the same time, decision-making in the case of a public client is also a decision made in a body, since the public clients have a multilevel and complex organizational structure, too. Thus, different units and peoples are involved in making decisions; nevertheless, politics could surround the project.

Basic Characteristics of the Clients' Decision-Making Process

As has been discussed, clients are organizational buyers. One of the most important characteristics of these buyers is that they make decisions by using standardized or *ad-hoc* decision-making mechanisms. Regarding the project cycle introduced in Chapter 2, one realizes that with respect to a contributor the marketing efforts should be focused on the awarding phase of the cycle. Making decisions on the capable tenderers and then making decisions on the best bid are concentrated in the awarding phase. The process of decision-making, which is a purchasing process for a client at the same time, has in any case many participants. There could be external consultants, as well, among these participants. The internal participants, representing different (functional) units of the client organization, could possess different formal and informal, i.e., *de jure* and *de facto* authorities. Making decisions is not a one-time, in-body event. Instead, the participants of the decision-making process work separately many times, not only in terms of time but also spatially. In this way, different participants join the process occasionally. Thus, each of the participants pursues his unit's interests and considerations and, willy-nilly, the individual standpoints also could come to the forefront. Based on the considerations mentioned earlier, each of the participants tries to exert influence on the others.

Nevertheless, the organizational decisions, owing to matching the different considerations, are more rational than those of the individual buyers. In spite of this, the final outcome of the decision-making process, because of the different and occasionally conflicting considerations and interests—e.g., operational safety versus costs—could be far from the best compromise. It is generally due to this fact that participants of the process act separately and, as a consequence, their authority with regard to the decision-making process could vary from time to time.

The more complex the project result to be implemented, the higher the number of the functional units or the participants involved in the process. Based on the roles played when making decisions, participants can be categorized as either influential participants or decision-makers. Those who are in some influential role could be further classified according to those who:

■ collect, analyze, and forward information (e.g., consultants, marketers, and so on—although most of the influential participants could have these tasks)

■ are in an indirect influential position (e.g., experts by means of fixing specifications that fit certain contributors)

■ are in a direct influential position (e.g., operators and users).

It is a common for those who are in some influential position to possess all of these influential roles with regard to a given project, often at the same time.

Unlike the influential participants, decision-makers differ from each other mainly based on their formal and informal authority. The decision itself is generally done by a permanent body, such as the board, or by an ad-hoc team.

The contributor has a fundamental need to hold a more or less clear picture about the client's decision-making mechanism, since the previously mentioned two main groups of participants in the client's decision-making process require different approaches throughout project marketing. Stressing the most important considerations in certain projects should dictate how influential participants will be approached. At the same time, decision-makers should be convinced that the contributor in question best suits the most important considerations and the consequences.

Factors That Shape the Client Decision-Making Characters

In a given situation, many different factors might exert influence on the decision-making mechanism and the associated decision-making process of a certain client. There are a couple of these factors that are present in any case and influence the outcome in some form. The following factors should be highlighted:

■ the client's strategic objective behind the project

■ the culture of operation characteristic to the client and her environment

■ the organizational structure and culture characteristic to the client

■ social and cultural traditions surrounding the client.

The Client's Strategic Objective behind the Project. The client does not view implementation of a certain project as the final goal. The final goal is to achieve strategic objectives through use of projects. As was pointed out in Chapter 1, the possible strategic objectives are partly determined by external environmental forces. The decisive forces may vary client to client, pending on the type of client in question.

Both individual and corporate clients are basically market-governed organizations; thus, they are motivated mainly by environmental factors characteristic to the market environment. As a result, creating and sustaining competitive advantages are central to their strategies. Nonetheless, in the course of initiating projects realizing strategies, other environmental factors, such as different regulations, environmental protection, and so on, should not be neglected.

Public clients, at the same time, are motivated mainly by the needs and expectations of the local or the wider public—for example, assembling traffic lights in order to decrease the number of accidents, building hospitals, and so on. The final goals in these cases are to satisfy some public need, although the extent to which such a need is satisfied could be limited by market considerations, such as the costs.

Another facet of this, especially in capital investment-engineering projects when the expected project result is a facility, is whether the client will operate the facility or some other organization and, furthermore, who the expected users are. For example, in the Old Country Project (see Chapter 6), the client operates the project result, while the users are private individuals. The local municipality generally operates a school building financed by the state, while its users are teachers and pupils. When these roles are separated, not only does the client have expectations regarding the project, but also both operators and users could have at least latent needs pertaining to the project result.

Considering the primary project targets again, there are tradeoffs between them (as was emphasized in Chapter 1). These primary targets are of different importance for the participants of the client's decision-making process, creating troublesome conflicts among the participants. Why is it important for a possible contributor to become acquainted with the considerations behind the project? The short answer to this question is the following: Possessing all of the related information would increase the potential to win. Bid invitations describe the project result to be implemented, but this documentation does not encompass the strategic considerations behind the project. Bid invitations also do not deal with the latent expectations of future operators and users. The clients' primary targets are also not manifested in some type of target-based financial settlement in every case, when it would be reasonable. As a corollary, contributors should investigate what lies behind a certain project, and their project marketing efforts should be focused on the considerations behind the project.

***The Culture of Operation Characteristic to the Client and Her
Environment.*** There are examples circulating among professionals
about tenderers who have not won bids even if they offered the
most up-to-date technical solution in their bids. A good case in
point is the Hungarian ÉLGÉP company, which offered a computer-
controlled mill in its bid for a Third-World client about twenty years
ago. This is an emerging problem when there is a gap between the
tenderer, the possible contributor, and the client in terms of the
culture of operation. Consequently, the client and her environment
do not possess the necessary skills. If these skills won't be gained
until project completion, the client would be inclined to select a
solution that is less up to date but can be operated safely.

On the other hand, using up-to-date technology generally results
in a decreasing need for workforce. At this point, there might be
some interrelationship between the operational culture and the
strategic objectives behind the project. If the final goal of a client
were to create jobs with the project, she would be inclined to select
a solution that would utilize less up-to-date technology but create
jobs at the same time.

Analyzing the culture of operation and the level of technical
development characteristic to the client's environment is of great
importance for a possible contributor when a turnkey-type contract
is utilized in the project strategy. Concentrating marketing efforts on
this area also would result in a favorable outcome for a contributor.

***The Organizational Structure and Culture Characteristic to the
Client.*** The authors of a Tavistock Institute publication have said
that "much design and even building work has proved to be
abortive because unresolved or unrecognized conflicts of interests
or objectives within the client system have only come to light after
the building process has been initiated ... " (1966, 39).

As was previously highlighted, owing to the characteristics of the
client and the project as a unique undertaking, the relevant decision-
making is a long and multidimensional process that includes many
participants. Participants of this process act in different roles, possessing different formal and informal authority, and based on different standpoints and interests that they try to exert on the outcome.
Whether or not the final outcome of the process is an acceptable
compromise for most of the participants largely depends on the cen-
tralized or decentralized character of the client organization and the
interpersonal communication skills of the participant. Both are
determined to a great extent by the organizational culture in the
wider sense.

Thus, it is worth the trouble for the possible contributors to
devote time and effort to investigating the clients' organizational
structure and the interpersonal relationships characteristic of the

organization. We should mention here the personal characters of those who participate in the decision-making process. The individual characteristics, such as education, experience, age, and so forth, shine through the functional caste to which the person in question belongs and conversely, as well. In this way, the marketing tools could influence individual attitude, although the organizational culture has a decisive role in this respect; it can compensate for the disadvantageous effects of the contributors' marketing efforts.

Social and Cultural Traditions Surrounding the Client. These generally come to the forefront when the client and his possible contributors operate in radically different social and cultural environments. They influence not only the decision-making mechanism, but also exert a direct influence on the outcome of the process. Thus, it is wise for the contributors to be concerned with these circumstances. Therefore, it is not amazing for a tender bid submitted by a European tenderer to be refused by an Islamic client because the tenderer did not consider Islamic traditions with respect to a meat industry project. Possessing prudent information about such traditions can help avoid such a situation, and efforts devoted to elaborating the tender bid would not be abortive.

Implications for Managers

The usual implications aim to summarize and highlight the lessons deriving from a certain practice and approach or from applying some methodology. Instead of this, the following implications are built on the word *warning*. The underlying philosophy of this approach is the fact that project marketing in both senses—either from the point of view of the project client or the possible contributors—could become a tool for manipulation.

Most projects have winners and losers, and politics and rumors surround most projects. Given these circumstances, a project client can manipulate the interest groups with ease, especially those that pursue interests other then legally enforceable ones. Management innovation projects, such as business-process reengineering projects that frequently result in a decreasing need for workforce, are considerable cases in point. In such a case, the marketing tool of involvement would not be used without problems. A hired-out employee is not expected to enthusiastically participate in the project. As a result, there is a strong need for ethics in managing the project, especially when different project marketing tools are used to create support for the project.

Possible contributors also require ethics when they want to persuade a project client of their capabilities relevant to implementing the expected project result. Many information technology projects are negative examples in this respect; of course, there are positive examples, as well. Nonetheless, a couple of contributors may feel inclined to take advantage of inexperienced clients. With the help of creating some mystery when using the previously mentioned tools, the client's intention regarding participation in his own project as an active player would be eliminated soon.

Thus, *warning* has the following message for both project client and contributors: establish and maintain reliable communication. A client should establish and maintain reliable communication with the groups that have some vested interest in the project, while the contributor should ensure that reliable communication is exercised toward whomever is in an influential or decision-maker position in a client organization. Reliable communication is governed by ethical considerations.

Chapter Thirteen

Information Technology in Project Management

THE REALIZATION OF primary targets for most projects concerns the ability to manage time and progress, cost and cash flow, and quality and performance, while responding to risk at the same time. The project manager therefore requires a tool to assist in decision-making, primarily in terms of the time and cost components of the project. Tools are also required to assist in the coordination of the project team, and these tools should be readily available at any time, in any project stage, to aid in planning, monitoring, and controlling the project. As has been shown earlier in the book, particularly in Chapters 4, 8, and 9, information technology software tools are an inherent part of project management today. The information technology tools employed by the project manager may be classified into packages and systems.

The authors are aware that there are a number of computer-based project management *methodologies*. One of the best known is PRINCE (PRojects IN Controlled Environments), developed by the United Kingdom government's Centre for Information Systems. However, as this book concentrates on project management understanding, these methodologies will not be described or discussed within this chapter despite the clear information technology links.

Information Technology Background and Terminology

Productivity packages refer to the plethora of available software that enables the project manager to execute tasks more efficiently. They range from simple word-processing packages and personal information managers to electronic mail and videoconferencing systems. In the area of information storage and retrieval, database packages are evolving to allow intelligent storage and retrieval of data. Current approaches under consideration include data warehousing and case-based reasoning. Emerging technologies such as intranets, extranets, and the Internet are playing an increasingly important role in facilitating the acquisition and dissemination of project information.

Personal computer-based systems account for about 90 percent of project management software and provide by far the largest range of choice to the potential user. In general, personal computers run the Windows operating system, offering a common graphical user interface to the user. There are three main versions of Windows: Windows 3.x, Windows 95 (an upgrade, Windows 98, is due), and Windows NT. It should be noted that the versions are not forward compatible; thus, software developed for Windows 95 will not run on Windows 3.x, and similarly software developed for Windows NT will not run on Windows 95. However, there is limited backward compatibility, as Windows 3.x programs will run on Windows 95, although not on Windows NT. Windows 95 programs in turn will run on Windows NT.

The real price of computers is falling, and a wider group of computer-literate people now have access to them, which has lead to the increased use of computers, especially desktop and personal computers, in the project management process. Computers are fast and efficient tools for evaluating data, but it is important that the users not lose sight of the assumptions upon which software packages are based. The idea that if the computer has produced something, then it must be right is a belief held by too many people, and it is certainly not true. The output from a computer model is determined by the information input, which means that accurate and appropriate data is essential.

The project model is based upon restricted information, which often consists of the client or contractor's estimate for the project. As shown in Figure 13.1, the project manager can then perform simulations, that is apply changes to the model, to try and predict the outcome of the project in order to provide a more realistic basis for decision-making. It is essential that the model be kept up to date for the effective monitoring of actual progress. Any problems that may occur can then be more easily identified and necessary action taken to ensure that planned targets are achieved.

The terms *modeling* and *simulation* are frequently used when discussing the utilization of computers in the risk-management process; however, the distinction between these two terms is not always understood. In broad terms, modeling is the process of describing the project in a mathematical way, and simulation is the process of imposing real-life complications on the model and measuring the effects.

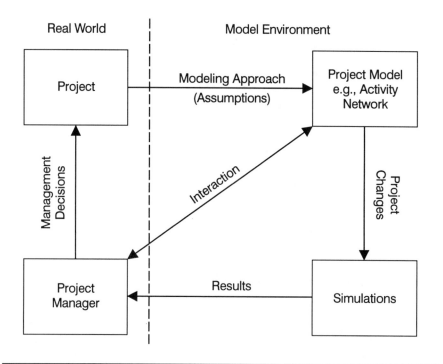

Figure 13.1   The Modeling Process

A model can be regarded as an approximation of reality. A model can never be a perfect representation of reality, as the actual reaction of the project to certain factors is unknown. However, it is important that the model be as realistic as possible to ensure that it will react in a similar way to the actual project when the real-life complications are added. It also should be balanced with the complexity of the model, which will increase its development time and level of interpretation of outputs required.

Simulation involves testing and experimentation with models, rather than with the real system. The models employed are representations of an object, system, or idea in some form other than that of the entity itself. The computer is a powerful aid to this activity, and this is a reason for the recent increase in simulation-based methods.

Within the sphere of project management, one is principally concerned with the time and cost effects of investment decisions and management actions, and mathematics is the best language for to expressing these parameters. The third principal project parameter, quality, can usually only be expressed in qualitative terms; thus, quality is not included in risk management software.

A mathematical model will include constants, variables, parameters, constraints, and mathematical operators, and its purpose is either optimization or description. Optimization will seek to identify the course of action that either maximizes return or minimizes expenditure; the purpose of the descriptive approach is to provide insight into the project considered.

The Monte Carlo technique results in a very powerful tool for risk analysis. Several software packages exist on the market with this combination. The influence-diagram method is a very flexible way of building the risk model, and it allows one to add all of risks to the model, not only those affecting time and cost estimates. The modeling processes also force the project manager to consider and measure the effect of external risks, which is usually much more important than the uncertainties that are a natural part of the estimates.

Project Management Applications

Most project management software is based on some form of mathematical model, most commonly a network. The project manager is concerned with three key factors: time, cost, and quality. As specifications and contractual procedures can largely control quality, the mathematical model is required to represent the interrelationship between the other two factors. The model is based upon a real project, often the client's estimate, and then simulation, the changing of the model, is used to try to assess the future outcome of the real project.

The basic objectives of project planning systems are to:

- create an accurate model of the project
- keep the model up to date
- make it easy to use and interactive
- facilitate the clear presentation of project information.

A typical structure is shown in Figure 13.2, but all good planning software should be capable of being used to see what has happened during the last review period, plan how to proceed, prepare a revised model, and distribute information.

In general, project-planning software operate in the following way, with a degree of sophistication in the data handling varying from package to package. A user models a project in terms of tasks and network logic; the system calculates timing and criticality of tasks; and the user defines resource usage of each task with associated costs. The system then aggregates resource-usage-per-time measure and, if the system is capable, optimizes this usage. Project models may be developed and used at various stages of the project.

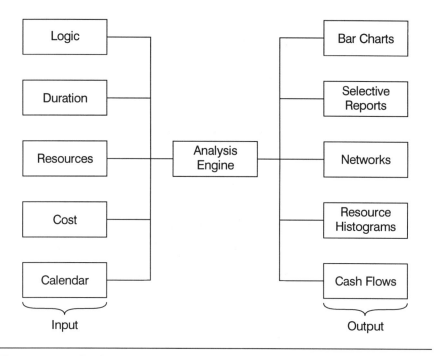

Figure 13.2   Project Planning System Functionality

Appraisal or Project Preparation Stage Modeling

Project appraisal is a process of investigation, review, and evaluation undertaken as the project or alternative concepts of the project are defined. The project evaluation should involve judgments about the likelihood of occurrence of the noncontrollable variables, calculation of a whole set of possible outcomes or returns for each project, and criteria for choosing among projects on the basis of the possible return. A project model at this stage is dominated by uncertainty; with little information likely to be available, it should be a simple network model with no more than fifty activities. The main resources should be allocated to the activities, along with cost and revenue.

Research has shown that for appraisal-stage simulations, the program should fulfill the following requirements:

- network modeling facilities
- flexibility in resource and cost allocation
- discounted cash-flow technique
- flexible risk-modeling module
- reporting facilities
- import/export functions.

If all of these options are not available within one package, the option of linking a number of packages should be considered.

Implementation or Construction/Erection Stage Modeling

The success and profitability of a contract will depend upon the ability of a contractor to manage and control time, cost, and quality effectively for labor and plant. An essential starting point in this control is the preparation of a realistic plan that sets out logically how the works are to be built, includes some contingency for unexpected events, and sets achievable targets against which progress can be monitored. The activity network, with resources and costs allocated, should be sensitive to the impact of changes made to the time and cost components so that action can be taken to prevent delays and possible additional costs. The model should be dynamic, that is, able to change with time to reflect new circumstances and project progress. The following criteria should be met:

- detailed network modeling facilities
- detailed cost and resourcing facilities
- intelligent resource-scheduling options
- progress measurement
- reporting facilities
- import/export functions.

The increasing commercial pressure to achieve predetermined time and cost targets, combined with the power of the desktop computer, has led to a proliferation of project-management software packages. These programs vary widely in terms of their modeling flexibilities and simulation options but are designed to serve the same purpose, which is to provide project managers with the power to plan the time and cost out-turn in projects. All programs link time, cost, and the resources of the project and allow the project manager to interactively forecast the financial commitment for the project, as well as to assess a range of scenarios to reflect likely change and uncertainty.

As project management programs become more and more a part of the everyday life of the project manager, it is important for the project manager to possess knowledge and skills within the areas of computing, simulation and simulation methods, statistics, and mathematical modeling concepts. These are in addition to the traditional qualifications needed for successful project management. (This is developed in greater detail in Chapter 4 on planning.)

Risk management software (RMS) packages are most commonly based on the network technique and the critical path method; the theoretical basis goes back to the 1950s. The other two principal components are planning packages and estimating packages. These packages have achieved wider use than RMS packages for a number of reasons, including the ease of use and analytical simplicity of most planning and estimating packages and their wider applicability. Until recently, RMS was only considered necessary when projects perceived as high risk were being appraised. This remains the case in many instances, although the increasing evaluation of projects over their entire lifetimes and a focus on political and financial risks over technical risks has promoted the use of RMS. (These programs are discussed in more detail in Chapter 9 on risk.)

Criteria for Software Selection

Evaluating programs by using them to model and simulate projects is in most cases very time consuming and inefficient. Typically, the project manager could be asked to base a selection on a range of brochures and demonstration versions of project management packages. Mistakes can be made at this stage, and a rational selection procedure is needed.

The selection of project management software needs to be based on both subjective and objective information. A method of integrating this information is to use decision analysis, which permits quantitative evaluation of the various courses of action to find the best possible program based on the project manager's needs. Decision analysis provides not only the philosophical foundations, but also a logical and quantitative procedure for decision-making.

Clearly, adoption of a rational selection procedure would be beneficial, and one method of doing this is using a decision table. This permits quantitative evaluation of the various courses of action to find the best possible action, based on the project manager's needs. A decision table enables the project manager to identify needs, then test software packages, and score the performance of each of the programs under consideration. The points scored are added, and the most feasible program should then be the one with the highest program rate. The choice of criteria and weightings will vary from user to user and by the sophistication of the decision table adopted.

In a decision table, one usually has a number of superfactors, which are the most important criteria, and then divides them into a number of relevant subfactors. The superfactors are given weightings relative to each other, and the subfactors are similarly assigned subweights, typically between one and five. Each of the factors is then given a range or score against which relative performance can be expressed, usually as "x/10". An overall rating for each program under assessment can then be calculated. Typically, potential criteria for superfactors may include:

- ease of use
- graphics
- functionality
- cost.

Each of the superfactors can then be divided into a number of subfactors:

- ease of use—interactive charting, four separate outlines, and complete customization
- graphics—customizable Gantt chart, cost/resource, PERT, and work breakdown structure (WBS) charts for clear portrayal of project data WYSIWYG reporting and presentation (WBS is sometimes referred to as PBS, or project breakdown structure.)
- functionality—advanced tools for scheduling, resource management, costing, and progress tracking and evaluation, as well as multiproject management
- cost—purchase price, license for networking and maintenance, staff training, and technical support and updating.

The choice of factors will vary widely. Large companies with considerable in-house computing experience very often have specialist-integrated programs for performing project management tasks, which would prove too expensive for smaller organizations, and hence may only purchase specialist packages. One of the future challenges for software producers is to create flexible programs for planning, estimating, control, accounting, procurement, and risk analysis with common interfaces. The trend though seems to be to impress users by emphasizing the user-interface and the screen graphics by creating endless view-screens and numerous ways of inputting data instead of increasing the time and cost-modeling flexibility, simplifying the simulation options, and improving program communication and program heuristics.

Artificial Intelligence and Knowledge-Based Systems and Case-Based Reasoning

The use of intelligent systems is increasing in project management. In the early days of artificial intelligence, it was sometimes stated that the ideal subject for this type of program was a topic with precise and fixed data, strict logic, and a finite number of predetermined questions that any user would like to pose. Hence, a bus timetable would be ideal. The sector has improved considerably, and many types of data and problems from project-delay management to contract administration have artificial intelligence/knowledge-based system decision-support systems. However, project management, with its focus on the earliest stages of a project with high degrees of uncertainty and a balance of *human*—that is subjective and factual—objective decision-making has found these systems to be of limited value.

One area of possible software development is the use of case-based reasoning, which is an emerging technology in artificial intelligence that solves problems by adapting solutions that were used to solve previous problems. This approach offers a paradigm similar to the way people solve problems. In practice, human experts are not systems of rules; they are a collection of expertise and experiences. When dealing with problems in the real world, they are often reminded of a previous similar problem, hence the attraction of adopting a program that reuses or modifies experience.

The concept of case-based reasoning (CBR) is relatively simple. Decision-makers' previous experiences are extracted and stored as cases in a case base. Given the details of a new case, the CBR system searches its case base for an existing case that exactly matches the input specification. The solution of the retrieved case is used to solve the problem without further modification if the new and retrieved cases are the same. If, however, there are no identical cases, the system retrieves the cases that offer the best match or closest fit to the input situation. Since the best matching cases may not properly reflect the new problem, the solutions of the retrieved cases may need to be adapted before they become useful. The new solution is used to solve the current problem, and it is then stored in the case base to improve the system, assisting it to learn about the problem.

Another usage of information technology that is increasingly important to project managers is the process model. This type of model depicts the primary activities and interactions between the associated information and material flows, and was developed as the IDEF0 methodology for activity modeling by the United States Airforce in 1991. The IDEF0 modeling technique provides a graphical structure and nomenclature, which facilitates the capture of functional relationships between activities involving different processes.

The main building block of an IDEF0 model is the activity box, which represents an activity. As an example, the order fulfillment process for structural steelwork is shown in Figure 13.3. Information and material flows are depicted by an associated set of input, control, output, and mechanism arrows. The order fulfillment activity's input is a processed order producing an erected structure. The activity is constrained by the requirements of the associated contract documents and applicable standards, personnel, and equipment forming the mechanism that executes the activity. The model captures an increasing level of detail in a hierarchical manner, through the decomposition of activities into more detailed diagrams.

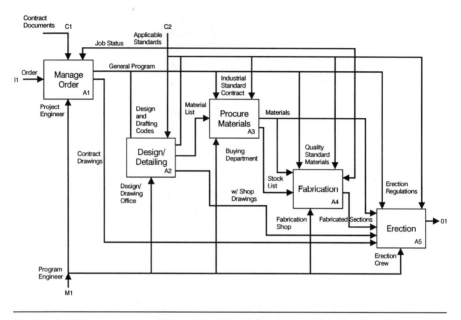

Figure 13.3   Decomposition of the Fabrication Activity

In developing the process model, interviews with experts usually form the main source of knowledge, while a limited amount of data can be acquired from relevant literature. Details on current activities, their sequence, and associated information flows are usually easily obtained; however, it may prove more difficult to establish an underlying rationale for the process other than custom and practice.

Chapter Fourteen

Project Management— The Future

THE CONCLUDING CHAPTER represents some of the authors' observations of the changes and developments in the theory and practice of project management in many countries, disciplines, and industry sectors over the last few years. It discusses some of these trends and reflects on the earlier chapters of the book to identify best practice and provide guidance to the new project manager who will be faced with the immediate problems of tomorrow. The former serves as a prelude to a shorter section considering the authors' thoughts on a vision of the future role and nature of project management. The chapter concludes with some speculations on the continuing use of project management in business.

Growth of Project Management

Although the functions of project management have been carried out on all successful projects ever undertaken, the role or existence of project management has not always been recognized as a discrete discipline. All clients and contributors have had to plan and control their respective roles in projects; manage the technology axis of the project management cycle; and organize and motivate the human axis of the project management cycle.

In the 1960s, planning techniques and methodologies were recognized as being important, particularly in the control of time. Later, it was realized that there are significant relationships between time and cost. While many regarded this as a natural extension of engineering or operations management, a few recognized the initial understanding of a separate discipline of project management. The concentration in the beginning was on tools and techniques that could be used by the project manager to address specific problems and produce *an answer*. The following twenty-five years saw the continued evolution and growth of project management as an integrated philosophy to pursue project success from conception to decommissioning.

These developments prompted the growth of professional institutes and associations: the Project Management Institute in the United States, the Association for Project Management in the United Kingdom, Nordnet in the Scandinavian countries, and many others, all under the world *umbrella* of the International Project Management Association (IPMA). Professional organizations promote the development of the discipline, share best practice, and disseminate information as a basis for innovation. Now the majority of businesses around the world seem to employ project managers, to manage by projects, and to be convinced of the role of project management.

Practice of Project Management

One of the guiding themes of this book is to assist the new project manager in taking that important step up from being *one of the team* to the key role of project manager. The book has been written at a strategic and business level, and does not go into the detail of every tool or technique mentioned. Some of these will already be familiar to the reader; others can be followed up in the helpful list of references provided at the end of the book.

It is important to understand the concepts and philosophy of project management, and the book commences with two chapters providing a context for an appreciation of the role of project management and the function of a project manager within an organization. They also pointed out the wider recognition of the dynamics of the project life cycle.

Some of the biggest changes in project management have occurred in the implementation stages of projects, with more and more of the project management activity being brought in at the earliest possible time in the project. In the execution of a major project, it used to be that each phase had its own manager or director, and there was little continuity of information or management throughout the project. This method has now been demonstrated to be at best wasteful and at worst a direct source of interface problems and inefficient management. Today, the project manager and team will be appointed at the earliest possible date after conception of the project idea. The most important work is completed at the front end of the project, at a time when change can have profound effects but costs relatively little to make. Chapter 3 on project formation addressed this issue in some detail and advocated the use of project structures and function vehicles.

The growth of information technology systems has facilitated the communication of project information and the sharing of information on which to base decisions. Chapter 4 considered planning and the role of information technology in the evolution of a project. The management role of planning was discussed, and the real-world problems of time, resource, and money constraints on projects were analyzed. This led into Chapters 5 and 6, dealing with project strategy, viewed by the authors as a means for allocating those risks and responsibilities associated with the primary project targets. This view is a positive view, and both advantages and potential disadvantages were highlighted. Chapter 6 also considered decision-making and problem solving in relation to the project profile and the client profile, including one of the most important project decisions: the selection of contract and contractor.

The increasing trend toward privatization in both developed and developing countries means that many major projects formerly funded by public funds through direct taxation are now being considered as vehicles for private finance. Chapter 7 investigated some of the additional problems for the project manager undertaking work of this type.

Returning to more conventional project management elements, Chapters 8 and 9 dealt with project control and project risk management, respectively. Here again, the book addressed the role and function rather than specific tools and techniques. Risk management is a vast topic and extremely important for project management. The chapters gave emphasis to the choice of analytical methodologies, the relationship with investment appraisal, and an appreciation of the underlying philosophies. Chapter 10 reviewed the selection of an appropriate organizational structure for any given project.

In the concluding three chapters, the book considered the meaning of success, the role of marketing, and the relationship between project management and information technology. These are important and relevant issues but can only be engaged once the fundamentals addressed in the earlier chapters have been satisfactorily resolved. Time does not stand still; project management recognizes time dynamics as inherent to projects, and although the basics described in the book should hold good for the short- to medium-term future, it is interesting to consider the future.

Recent Trends

The need for the project management approach in the future is and will continue to be demonstrated by the continuing failure of projects to consistently meet time, cost, and quality deadlines. To meet these goals each and every time appears to be a tall order, but it is really the project management equivalent of total quality management. The long-term objective of satisfying all primary project targets has to be approached with continuing improvement in project management performance in business. The adopted approach toward sharing of best practices in business processes and the facility with which the transition from strategic objective to being a part of an organization's day-to-day operation is made also are increasingly important in terms of competitiveness.

In the United Kingdom, a Code of Practice for Project Management, British Standard 6079, was issued in 1996 to provide guidance to general managers, budget managers, and support staff. British Standard 6079 draws attention to management problems encountered in different project environments and presents possible solutions to these problems. Projects are regarded as nonrepetitive and tend to have significant unique features. The project is always defined by characteristics that make it different from other similar projects. Unique features of projects may not be reflected in the physical features of the project, but in project organization or in the process of construction. All dependencies of the project to other external systems are sources of risk, as well as uncertainty.

Projects should be approved in return for undertaking to deliver specified quantified results within predetermined quality, safety, and health parameters. The authorization should leave no doubt that results will need to be delivered. Projects are usually in the hands of a temporary team and may be subject change as the work progresses. Each project has its own life cycle; each phase has certain distinguishing features compared with other phases. Changing project organization is expected to become more important. The current pace of change is causing corporate management to undertake more tasks with unfamiliar characteristics. The strategic decisions may be expressed as the undertaking of a series of projects. British Standard 6079 acknowledges that project management is a way of answering these changes in the economic environment for the survival of a company.

The public is becoming more critical of the performance of projects. In order to minimize these objections, project authorization has to be carried out quickly. This indicates that although the project sponsor is not playing any direct part in the project, he has the authority and must respond quickly in order to be successful. Effective project management requires the motivation of people in addition to the planning, organizing, implementing, and controlling aspects of a project life cycle.

The British Standard differentiates between a project manager and a task owner. The task owner is defined as "a person bound by a legal contract with the project manager." The project manager should obtain commitments from task owners to undertake work. Commitments may be quantified by a date beyond which the task owner deserves the right to withdraw any commitment that has not been fully accepted. Equally, the project manager has the right to negotiate any objections to the plans. The form of these negotiations will depend upon a legal relationship between the project manager and task owner, and the agreement could be informal or a legally binding contract. Equally, a contract can place restrictions on this relationship and reduce the authority of the project manager.

British Standard 6079 also notes the importance of managing change. It recognizes that human resources will be most affected by any change. Change within the project organizational structure is likely to occur during the project life cycle. It is therefore essential to prepare people, the human resources, for change. Effective management involves developing an understanding of the current phase and an awareness of the next phase and moving the organization through this transition. Staff should be given descriptions of all the roles in the next phase. Communication is important in providing feedback on operating procedures and providing information to inform future decision-making.

The United Kingdom Association for Project Management Body of Knowledge defines *project* as a temporary endeavor undertaking to create a unique product or service. Every project has a definite beginning and a definite end. *Unique* means that the product or service is different in some distinguishing way from any other products or services.

It is recognized that knowledge is different for each different type of project in the project life cycle. Dividing the project into phases provides better management control and appropriate links to the ongoing operations of the business organization. Projects are usually part of a larger organization, which will include the project in terms of organizational systems, cultures style, and structure. It is also recognized that the organizational structure will be either project orientated or nonproject orientated. Naturally, the project manager's authority will be lowest within a functional organization and highest in a project-oriented organization. The project context will be highly important for stakeholder expectations. Project managers, individuals, and organizations are largely involved in a project in which interests may be positively or negatively affected as a result of its execution. Project management teams must identify all stake-holders, determine their needs and expectations, and then manage those expectations to ensure a successful outcome.

Initiation is recognized as the process of formally identifying that a new project exists, and acknowledgement of what links the project to the ongoing work of the performing organization. Projects are typically authorized as a result of one or more of the following: market demand, business needs, customer request, technological advances, or legal requirements. Problems, opportunities, or business requirements are stimuli for project initiation. The gap in regard to project skills and project integration management can be an important part of the developing project. Project management concentrates on initiation, skill planning, scope definition, and scope change. Project integration recognizes the complex project and the processes within the project. Projects in different phases in the life cycle require different inputs and use different processes to produce different outputs.

In the event of uncertainty in the future development of a project, project strategy provides a framework for project management and offers alternative procedures; approaches are planning methods due to achieve project outcome. All project leaders' strategies for successful completion should comply with company business, and utilize the appropriate sections of this book to identify effective and efficient ways to produce the project. The trend in most developing technologies is to move from successful, if empirical, techniques and tools to a simplified, self-contained *black-box* theory and ultimately to the open, fully integrated *white-box* approach. Project management is currently somewhere between the black and white extremes, and innovations are implemented continuously.

Vision for Project Management

While vision is a part of predicting future behavior and performance, there are limits on its value. Business will be increasingly faced with competition for scarce resources, some of which may become so serious that they achieve national importance. Can project management still function in this environment?

It is always difficult to see into the future, but in essence this is what project management is about. To foresee the future of project management itself is even more of a challenge. However, a number of issues stand out. Business in general is moving toward operating the concept of sustainability, and this has implications for the wider contractual environment and the role of the public or society in projects.

Bibliography

Ahuja, H., S. P. Dozzi, and S. M. Abourizk. 1994. *Project Management,* 2d ed. John Wiley & Sons.

Allen, T., R. Katz, J. Grady, and N. Slavin. 1988. Project Team Aging and Performance: The Roles of Project and Functional Manager. *R&D Management* 18 (4).

Ashley, D. 1981. Construction Project Risks: Mitigation and Management. In *The World of Project Management 1981 Proceedings.* Drexel Hill, PA: Project Management Institute.

———. New Trends in Risk Management. In *New Approaches in Project Management: Proceedings of the 10ᵗʰ International Expert Seminar.* Zurich: INTERNET.

Ashley, D., C. Lurie, and E. Jaselskis. 1987. Determinants of Construction Project Success. *Project Management Journal* 18 (2).

Baker, N., D. Murphy, and D. Fischer. 1982. Factors Affecting Project Success. In *Handbook of Project Management.* New York: Van Nostrand Reinhold.

Balck, H. 1994. Projects as Elements of a New Industrial Pattern: A Division of Project Management. In *Global Project Management Handbook,* eds. D. I. Cleland and R. Gareis. New York: McGraw-Hill.

Barnes, M. 1981. Project Management by Motivation. In *The World of Project Management 1981 Proceedings.* Drexel Hill, PA: Project Management Institute.

———. 1989. Financial Control of Construction. In *Control of Engineering Projects,* 2d ed., ed. S. H. Wearne. London: Thomas Telford.

Baum, W. C. 1978. The World Bank Project Cycle. *Finance and Development* 15 (4).

Bergen, S. A. 1990. *R&D Management: Managing Projects and New Products.* Oxford: Basil Blackwell.

Berry, A. D. 1994. Dynamic Leadership through Project Management. In *Dynamic Leadership through Project Management.* INTERNET '94 12th World Congress Proceedings. Vol. 1. Oslo, Norway.

Briner, W. and C. Hastings. 1994. The Role of Projects in the Strategy Process. In *Global Project Management Handbook,* eds. D. I. Cleland and R. Gareis. New York: McGraw-Hill.

British Standard 6079. 1997. Project Management.

Buchanan, D. A. 1991. Vulnerability and Agenda: Context and Process in Project Management. *British Journal of Management* 2 (3).

Burger, R., and M. Fisher. 1986. An Expert System for Project Organization. In *New Approaches in Project Management. Proceedings of the 10th International Expert Seminar*. Zurich: INTERNET.

Carrier, A. 1987. Sequential Steps in Project Execution. *International Journal of Project Management* 5 (1).

Chapman, C. B., D. F. Cooper, and M. J. Page. 1987. *Management for Engineers*. London: John Wiley & Sons.

CIRIA SP 15. 1981. *A Client's Guide to Design and Build*. Special Publication SP 15. London: CIRIA.

Cleland, D. I. 1994. *Project Management: Strategic Design and Implementation*, 2d ed. New York: McGraw-Hill.

Cleland, D. I., and W. R. King. 1975. *Systems Analysis and Project Management*, 2d ed. New York: McGraw-Hill.

Clough, R. H. 1972. *Construction Project Management*. New York: Wiley-Interscience.

Cocke-Davies, T. 1994. Project Management and the Management of Change. In *Dynamic Leadership through Project Management*. INTERNET '94 12th World Congress Proceedings, Vol. 1., Oslo, Norway.

Cooper, D. F., and C. B. Chapman. 1987. *Risk Analysis for Large Projects: Models, Methods, and Cases*. John Wiley & Sons.

Csath, M. 1990. *Stratégiai vezetés-vállalkozás*. Budapest: KJK.

Demarco, T. 1979. Structured Analysis and System Specification. Prentice Hall.

Derkinderen, F. G. 1979. *Project Set Strategies*. Boston: Nijhoff.

Engwall, M. 1990. Flat Corporate Organizations: A Complex Environment for Engineering Projects. In *Management by Projects*. Proceedings of the 10th INTERNET World Congress on Project Management, MANZ Verlag, Vienna.

Enhassi, A., and R. Burges. 1990. The Leadership Style of Construction: Managers in Multi-National Organizations in the Middle East: An Empirical Analysis. In *Management by Projects*. Proceedings of the 10th INTERNET World Congress on Project Management. MANZ Verlag, Vienna.

Eskerod, P. 1994. The Hidden Side of Project Orientation. In *Dynamic Leadership through Project Management*. INTERNET '94 12th World Congress Proceedings, Vol. 1., Oslo, Norway.

Franke, A. 1987. Risk Analysis in Project Management. *International Journal of Project Management* 5 (1) (Feb.).

Gabriel, E. 1990. The Future of Project Management—The New Model. In *Management by Projects*. Proceedings of the 10th INTERNET Congress on Project Management, MANZ Verlag, Vienna.

Gareis, R. 1990. *Handbook of Management by Projects*. Vienna: Manz Verlag.

———. 1994. Management by Projects: Specific Strategies, Structures and Cultures of the Project-Oriented Company. In *Global Project Management Handbook*, eds. D. I. Cleland and R. Gareis. New York: McGraw-Hill.

Gold, B. 1991. Strengthening R&D and Its Integration with Corporate Operations. *OMEGA International Journal of Management Science* 19 (1).

Goodman, L. J., and R. N. Love. 1980. *Project Planning and Management: An Integrated Approach.* New York: Pergamon Press.

Görög, M. 1996. *Általános projektmenedzsmentbe.* Budapest: Aula Kiadó.

――――. 1993. *Bevezetés a projektmenedzsmentbe.* Budapest: Aula Kiadó.

――――. 1995. Client-Oriented Strategic Project Management. In *INTERNET Symposium Proceedings.* St. Petersburg, Russia.

――――. 1994. How to Find Sound Contract Strategy. In *Dynamic Leadership through Project Management.* INTERNET '94 World Congress Proceedings, Vol. 2, Oslo, Norway.

Harberger, A. 1972. *Project Evaluation.* London: Macmillan.

Harrison, F. L. 1990. Is the Federal Organization Set to Replace the Matrix Organization as the Project Organization of the 90's? In *Management by Projects.* Proceedings of the 10th INTERNET Congress on Project Management, MANZ Verlag, Vienna.

Harvey, R. 1990. Managing Across the Matrix. In *Management by Projects.* Proceedings of the 10th INTERNET Congress on Project Management, MANZ Verlag, Vienna.

Hayes, R. W., J. G. Perry, and P. A. Thompson. 1983. *Management Contracting.* CIRIA Report 100. London: CIRIA.

Horgan, M. 1984. *Competitive Tendering for Engineering Projects.* London: Spon.

Johnson, G., and K. Scholes. 1993. *Exploring Corporate Strategy: Text and Cases,* 3d ed. New York-London: Prentice Hall.

Kerzner, H. 1992. *Project Management,* 4th ed. Van Nostrand Reinhold.

Kharbanda, O. P., and E. A. Stallworthy. 1991. *Cost Control.* Institution of Chemical Engineers.

Knutson, J., and I. Bitz. 1991. *Project Management: How to Plan and Manage Successful Projects.* New York: AMACOM.

Kotler, P. 1997. *Marketing Management: Analysis, Planning, Implementation and Control,* 9th ed. Englewood Cliffs, NJ: Prentice Hall.

Levitt, R. 1981. Superprojects and Superheadaches: Balancing Technical Economies of Scale Against Managing Diseconomies of Size and Complexity. In *The World of Project Management 1981 Proceedings.* Drexel Hill, PA: Project Management Institute.

Levy, S. M. 1996. *Build Operate Transfer.* New York: John Wiley & Sons.

Lock, D. 1992. *Project Management,* 5th ed. Aldershot: Gower.

Marsh, P. D. V. 1981. *Contracting for Engineering and Construction Projects,* 2d ed. Aldershot: Gower.

Merna, T., and N. J. Smith. 1996. *Guide to the Preparation and Evaluation of Build-Own-Operate-Transfer (BOOT) Project Tenders.* Asia Law and Practice.

Merna, T., and N. J. Smith, eds. 1996. *Projects Procured by Privately Financed Concession Contracts.* Manchester: UMIST Project Management Group.

Miller, E. J., and A. K. Rice. 1967. *Systems of Organization.* London: Tavistock Publications.

Mintzberg, H. 1983. *Structure in Fives: Designing Effective Organizations.* Englewood Cliffs, NJ: Prentice Hall.

Morris, P. W. G., and G. H. Hough. 1987. *The Anatomy of Major Projects: A Study of the Reality of Project Management*. Chichester: John Wiley & Sons.

Murray, W., and H. Moody. 1981. The Project Manager in the Marketing Professional Service. In *World of Project Management 1981 Proceedings*. Drexel Hill, PA: Project Management Institute.

NEDO. 1990. *Private Participation in Infrastructure*. London: National Economic Development Council.

Park, W. R. 1966. *The Strategy of Contracting for Profit*. Englewood Cliffs, NJ: Prentice Hall.

Pearson, A. W. 1990. Planning and Control in Research and Development. *OMEGA International Journal of Management Science* 18 (6).

Perry, J. G. 1985. The Development of Contract Strategies for Construction Projects. UMIST Ph.D. Thesis.

Perry, J. G., and P. A. Thompson. 1982. *Target and Cost-Reimbursable Construction Contracts*. CIRIA Report 85. London: CIRIA.

Pike, A. 1982. *Engineering Tenders, Sales and Contracts: Standard Forms and Procedures*. London: Spon.

Pinto, J. K. 1986. Project Implementation: A Determination of Its Critical Success Factors, Moderators, and Their Relative Importance across the Project Life Cycle. Dissertation, University of Pittsburgh.

Porter, M. E. 1979. How Competitive Forces Shape Strategy. *Harvard Business Review* 57 (2).

Project Management Institute Standards Committee. 1996. *A Guide to the Project Management Body of Knowledge*. Upper Darby, PA: Project Management Institute.

Robinson, J. 1987. Comparison of Tendering Procedures and Contractual Arrangements. *International Journal of Project Management* 5 (1).

Shaughnessy, Haydn, ed. 1996. *Project Finance in Europe*. New York: John Wiley & Sons.

Shtub, A., J. F. Bard, and S. Globerson. 1994. *Project Management*. Prentice Hall International.

Smith, N. J. 1995. *Project Cost Estimating*. London: Thomas Telford Ltd.

———. 1996 Reprint. *Engineering Project Management*. Blackwell Science.

Smith, N. J., ed. 1998. *Managing Risks in Construction Projects*. Blackwell Science.

Smith, N. J., and O. Husby. 1991. Application of Project Management Software in Construction Projects. *Nordnet '91 Transactions*. Trondheim.

Tavistock Institute. 1966. *Interdependence and Uncertainty*. London: Tavistock Publications.

Thompson, J. 1967. *Organizations in Action*. New York: McGraw-Hill.

Thompson, P. A. 1981. *Organization and Economics of Construction*. London: McGraw-Hill.

Thompson, P. A., and J. G. Perry. 1992. *Engineering Construction Risks*. London: Thomas Telford.

Turner, J. Rodney. 1995. *The Commercial Project Manager*. McGraw-Hill.

van den Honert, A. 1994. The Strategic Connection with Project Processes. In *Dynamic Leadership through Project Management*. INTERNET '94 12ᵗʰ World Congress Proceedings, Vol. 1. Oslo, Norway.

Vriethoff, W. J. 1986. Innovation in Project Management Approaches. In *New Approaches in Project Management. Proceedings of the 10ᵗʰ International Expert Seminar*. Zürich: INTERNET.

Walker, A. 1989. *Project Management in Construction*, 2d ed. Oxford: BSP Professional Books.

Ward, J. 1994. Drivers into Leaders—The Challenge Facing Many Project Managers. In *Dynamic Leadership through Project Management*. INTERNET '94 12ᵗʰ World Congress Proceedings, Vol. 1, Oslo, Norway.

Wearne, S. H. 1985. Matrix Management or Internal Contracts? *International Journal of Project Management* 3 (1) (Feb.).

———. 1994. Preparing for Privatized Project Management. *International Journal of Project Management* 12 (2).

———, ed. 1989. *Control of Engineering Projects*, 2d ed. London: Thomas Telford.

Webb, A. 1994. *Managing Innovative Projects*. London: Chapman & Hall.

Webster, F. M., Jr. 1994. We Don't Do Projects! In *Global Project Management Handbook*, D. I. Cleland and R. Gareis, eds. New York: McGraw-Hill.

Willard, E. P. 1994. The Superconducting Super Collider—The Demise of a Super Project. In *Dynamic Leadership through Project Management*. INTERNET '94 12ᵗʰ World Congress Proceedings, Vol. 1, Oslo, Norway.

Index

M

management contractor   65–67, 79, 137

manager of project managers   131
See also project director and project
manager

marketing, project   *See* project marketing

mathematical model   156, 158

matrix organizational structure(s)   120
See also functional matrix, project matrix,
strong matrix, and weak matrix

mission   3–4, 6–7, 142–44

modeling and simulation   154

Monte Carlo   110, 156

mutual adjustment   123–27

N

network analysis   48

nonrecourse finance   87–88, 93

O

operating function   28, 31–32, 34, 45, 71

operating management   2, 3, 6, 11

operating phase   24, 32–33, 36

organizational structure   2–3, 23, 35, 45,
115–17, 122–23, 125–28, 130–31
and marketing   146–48, 150
and the future   165, 167
linear-functional   116, 118, 125

P

planning and control cycle   47, 98

planning method selection   51

planning technique   47–49, 98, 163

postevaluation phase

postqualification

precedence diagram   48

prequalification   54, 69–70, 78–84, 89, 138,
140

primary project targets   10–12, 15, 21,
25–26, 39, 44, 50, 107, 118, 149
and project strategy   53–54, 58, 70–71,
73, 75, 84
and project success   133–37
and the future   165–66

private finance   85–86, 88, 94, 165

Private Finance Initiative   94

process model   161–62

program   4, 7, 47–49, 51, 82, 94, 102, 105,
154, 157–61

project client   *See* client, project

project cycle   17–19, 21–26, 32, 37, 39–40,
42–43, 53, 61, 92, 128, 130, 137
and marketing   147
and the future   169

project director   131
See also manager of project managers and
project manager

project failure   *See* project manager

project finance   86

project formation   15, 24, 27, 31, 37, 134,
165
phase   23–24, 53
preparation   10, 18–19, 21, 24–25, 34, 43,
77, 81, 128, 134, 144, 157–58, 171

project champion   95
See also project manager

project management
growth of   163–64
practice of   xi, 43, 163–64
recent trends   166
vision for   168

project manager   48, 51, 93–94, 97–98,
101–02, 117, 121, 135
and information technology   153–54,
156, 158–59
and risk   106, 108–09, 113–14
and success or failure   137–38
authority   4, 10, 116, 118–20, 127,
129–31, 147

strategy implementation   xi, 4, 6–7, 9, 15–16, 142

strong matrix   122
    See also project matrix

T

task   1, 29, 33, 44, 48, 93, 100, 117

task force   116, 118–22, 127–29
    See also project task-force organization

tendering   69–70, 78, 81–84
    invitation   82–84
    open   81–84
    procedure   54, 69, 78, 138
    selective   82–84
    serial   82
    two-tier tendering   82, 83, 84

time and cost constraint(s)   4, 6–7, 10, 14, 16, 18, 25, 39–40, 42, 44, 53, 137

turnkey contractor   63–64, 79, 80

U

uncertainty   17, 26–27, 40, 49–50, 77, 94, 97–98, 102, 105–06, 125, 128
    and information technology 157–58, 161
    and the future 166, 168

unit price   55, 77

V

vision   2–4, 6–7, 32, 163, 168

W

weak matrix   122
    See also functional matrix

Upgrade Your Project Management Knowledge with First-Class Publications from PMI

A Guide to the Project Management Body of Knowledge

The basic management reference for everyone who works on projects. Serves as a tool for learning about the generally accepted knowledge and practices of the profession. As "management by projects" becomes more and more a recommended business practice worldwide, the *PMBOK Guide* becomes an essential source of information that should be on every manager's bookshelf. Available in hardcover or paperback, the *PMBOK Guide* is an official standards document of the Project Management Institute.

ISBN: 1-880410-12-5 (paperback), 1-880410-13-3 (hardcover)

Interactive PMBOK Guide

This CD-ROM makes it easy for you to access the valuable information in PMI's *A Guide to the Project Management Body of Knowledge*. Features hypertext links for easy reference—simply click on underlined words in the text, and the software will take you to that particular section in the *PMBOK Guide*. Minimum system requirements: 486 PC, 8MB RAM, 10MB free disk space, CD-ROM drive, mouse or other pointing device, and Windows 3.1 or greater.

PMBOK Review Package

This "Box of Books" offers you a set of materials that supplements the *PMBOK Guide* in helping you develop a deeper understanding of the Project Management Body of Knowledge. These important and authoritative publications offer the depth and breadth you need to learn more about project integration, scope, time, cost, quality, human resources, communications, risk, and procurement management. Includes the following titles: *Project Management Casebook; Human Resource Skills for the Project Manager; Project and Program Risk Management; Quality Management for Projects & Programs; PMBOK Q&A; Managing the Project Team; Organizing Projects for Success;* and *Principles of Project Management.*

Managing Projects Step-by-Step ™

Follow the steps, standards, and procedures used and proven by thousands of professional project managers and leading corporations. This interactive multimedia CD-ROM based on PMI's *A Guide to the Project Management Body of Knowledge* will enable you to customize, standardize, and distribute your project plan standards, procedures, and methodology across your entire organization. Multimedia illustrations using 3-D animations and audio make this perfect for both self-paced training or for use by a facilitator.

PMBOK Q&A

Use this handy pocket-sized question-and-answer study guide to learn more about the key themes and concepts presented in PMI's international standard, *A Guide to the Project Management Body of Knowledge*. More than 160 multiple-choice questions with answers (referenced to the *PMBOK Guide*) help you with the breadth of knowledge needed to understand key project management concepts.

ISBN: 1-880410-21-4

PMI Proceedings Library CD-ROM

This interactive guide to PMI's Annual Seminars & Symposium Proceedings offers a powerful new option to the traditional methods of document storage and retrieval, research, training, and technical writing. Contains complete paper presentations from PMI '91–PMI '97. Full-text-search capability, convenient on-screen readability, and PC/Mac compatibility.

PMI Publications Library CD-ROM

Using state-of-the-art technology, PMI offers complete articles and information from its major publications on one CD-ROM, including *PM Network* (1991–97), *Project Management Journal* (1991–97), and *A Guide to the Project Management Body of Knowledge*. Offers full-text-search capability and indexing by *PMBOK Guide* knowledge areas. Electronic indexing schemes and sophisticated search engines help to find and retrieve articles quickly that are relevant to your topic or research area.

Also Available from PMI

Project Leadership from Theory to Practice
Jeffery K. Pinto, Peg Thoms, Jeffrey Trailer, Todd Palmer and Michele Govekar
ISBN: 1-880410-10-9 (paperback)

Annotated Bibliography of Project and Team Management
David I. Cleland, Gary Rafe and Jeffrey Mosher
ISBN: 1-880410-47-8 (paperback)
ISBN: 1-880410-57-5 (CD-ROM)

How to Turn Computer Problems into Competitive Advantage
Tom Ingram
ISBN: 1-880410-08-7 (paperback)

Achieving the Promise of Information Technology
Ralph Sackman
ISBN: 1-880410-03-6 (paperback)

Leadership Skills for Project Managers
Editors' Choice Series
Edited by Jeffrey Pinto and Jeffrey Trailer
ISBN: 1-880410-49-4 (paperback)

The Virtual Edge
Margery Mayer
ISBN: 1-880410-16-8 (paperback)

ABCs of DPC
PMI's Design-Procurement-Construction Specific Interest Group
ISBN: 1-880410-07-9 (paperback)

Project Management Casebook
Edited by David Cleland, Karen Bursic, Richard Puerzer, and A. Yaroslav Vlasak
ISBN: 1-880410-45-1 (paperback)

Project Management Casebook Instructor's Manual
Edited by David Cleland, Karen Bursic, Richard Puerzer, and A. Yaroslav Vlasak
ISBN: 1-880410-18-4 (paperback)

PMI Book of Project Management Forms
ISBN: 1-880410-31-1 (Spiral bound)
ISBN: 1-880410-50-8 (Diskette version 1.0)

Principles of Project Management
John Adams et al.
ISBN: 1-880410-30-3 (paperback)

Organizing Projects for Success
Human Aspects of Project Management Series, Volume 1
Vijay Verma
ISBN: 1-880410-40-0 (paperback)

Human Resource Skills for the Project Manager
Human Aspects of Project Management Series, Volume 2
Vijay Verma
ISBN: 1-880410-41-9 (paperback)

Managing the Project Team
Human Aspects of Project Management Series, Volume 3
Vijay Verma
ISBN: 1-880410-42-7 (paperback)

Earned Value Project Management
Quentin Fleming, Joel Koppelman
ISBN: 1-880410-38-9 (paperback)

Value Management Practice
Michel Thiry
ISBN: 1-880410-14-1 (paperback)

Decision Analysis in Projects
John Schuyler
ISBN: 1-880410-39-7 (paperback)

The World's Greatest Project
Russell Darnall
ISBN: 1-880410-46-X (paperback)

Power & Politics in Project Management
Jeffrey Pinto
ISBN: 1-880410-43-5 (paperback)

Best Practices of Project Management Groups in Large Functional Organizations
Frank Toney, Ray Powers
ISBN: 1-880410-05-2 (paperback)

Project Management in Russia
Vladimir I. Voropajev
ISBN: 1-880410-02-8 (paperback)

Experience, Cooperation and the Future:
The Global Status of the Project Management Profession
ISBN: 1-880410-04-4 (paperback)

A Framework for Project and Program Management Integration
R. Max Wideman
ISBN: 1-880410-01-X (paperback)

Quality Management for Projects & Programs
Lewis R. Ireland
ISBN: 1-880410-11-7 (paperback)

Project & Program Risk Management
R. Max Wideman
ISBN: 1-880410-06-0 (paperback)

Order online at www.pmibookstore.org

To order by mail:
PMI Headquarters
Four Campus Boulevard
Newtown Square, Pennsylvania 19073-3299 USA

Or call 610-356-4600 or fax 610-356-4647